*Dynamics of*
*Christian Adult Education*

# Dynamics of Christian Adult Education

## ROBERT S. CLEMMONS

ABINGDON PRESS

*New York* • *Nashville*

DYNAMICS OF CHRISTIAN ADULT EDUCATION

*Copyright* © *MCMLVIII by Abingdon Press*

All rights in this book are reserved.
No part of the book may be reproduced in any
manner whatsoever without written permission of
the publishers except brief quotations embodied in
critical articles or reviews. For information address
Abingdon Press, Nashville 2, Tennessee.

*Library of Congress Catalog Card Number:* 58-8122

Scripture quotations designated R.S.V. are from the
Revised Standard Version of the Bible and are copyright
1946 and 1952 by the Division of Christian Education
of the National Council of the Churches of Christ in
the U.S.A.

*Family Portrait* is copyright 1937, 1939, by Lenore
Coffee and William Joyce Cowen. Copyright, 1940
(Acting Edition), by Lenore Coffee and William
Joyce Cowen. Selection reprinted by permission of the
authors and Samuel French, Inc. Application for the
right to perform or reproduce any portion of *Family
Portrait*, or the entire play, must be made to French,
at 25 West 45th Street, New York 36, N. Y., or 7623
Sunset Blvd., Hollywood 46, Calif., or, if in Canada,
to Samuel French (Canada) Ltd., 27 Grenville St.,
Toronto, Ont.

B

SET UP, PRINTED, AND BOUND BY THE
PARTHENON PRESS, AT NASHVILLE,
TENNESSEE, UNITED STATES OF AMERICA

TO MY MOTHER

*First Teacher of Religion*

# *Preface*

THIS BOOK IS THE PRODUCT OF HUNDREDS OF MEETINGS WITH teachers and leaders of adult classes in Protestant churches throughout the United States. These persons represent one of the largest bands of volunteer workers in the country. Each week they give over a million hours of service that other adults may learn more of the Christian way of life. This devotion represents one of the most dynamic expressions of faith through service that is to be witnessed anywhere.

During the past decade three major movements have come together to create a new forward thrust in Christian adult education. Group dynamics enables leaders to discover anew the power of small groups thinking and working together. America no longer doubts or debates that adults can learn; they know that they must in this new age of technology and atomic power. They are demanding many new opportunities and procedures in adult education. Moreover, the lay movement is reassessing the meaning of its faith and finding new roles of leadership in the church. The interaction of these three factors causes a dynamic situation in Christian adult education.

It would be impossible to recall and mention all those who have had a part in influencing my thinking as I have written this book. They are too numerous to mention. However, I would like to express my gratitude to my wife Beatrice, manuscript critic par excellence, and to Mrs. Shelton Luton and Mrs. Fred Sloan, who typed the manuscript.

ROBERT S. CLEMMONS

# Contents

# CHAPTER I

## *A New Era for Adult Students*

EACH YEAR HALF THE ADULT POPULATION IN THE UNITED States participates in some kind of adult education enterprise. This is something new under the sun! The old notion that the average American has the intelligence of a twelve-year-old simply isn't true. The reason? He kept on learning. He liked it and he is still working at it.

Of course, this doesn't mean that the average American adult packs up his books and goes trekking off to some educational institution. Some do, but most adult education is more informal. It does mean that over fifty million adults belong to clubs, attend classes, participate in discussion groups, go to lectures, take correspondence courses, meet with parents' groups, attend night schools, learn how to freeze peaches, and go to church school on Sunday to learn more about the faith they profess.

The largest number of adults in America in any educational enterprise is in the churches. Fifteen million of them! That's twice as many as you will find in all the many agricultural extension services, for instance. It shows that persons are seeking a new quality to their lives. Getting more gadgets is not enough. They want to *be* something—more mature Christians.

Why? Why has this change taken place in America since World War II? Perhaps there are many reasons.

An elderly lady said that when her husband died life seemed empty. She could exist economically but she wanted some meaning for her lonely existence. In a church group of older adults she found the answer, a personal answer.

When his job became obsolete, a middle-aged man realized that he could learn a new skill. He learned to relate himself to people in such a way that others began to seek him out as a person with whom they would like to talk things over. A man whose actions are guided by basic Christian ethics and who is spiritually sensitive to the needs of others is a real asset in any business. He learned this in the church school.

A young physicist discovered that his college views of God did not mean much to inquisitive four-year-old Junior, so he joined a parents' group of young adults to learn how to communicate the love of God to his child in such a way that it was related to the child's own level of development.

## The Church Can Help

Adults are participating in the educational program of the church because they discern something of increasing worth within it. It meets the deepest needs of their souls. It has spiritual value. It puts life together in a way that gives it meaning. It quickens within them a sense of their worth. It is relevant. It helps them in learning how to relate themselves to others as persons. It is redemptive. It helps them change under their own self-direction as they discern more clearly the spirit of Christ.

This new demand for lifetime learning presents the church with its greatest opportunity in this century. Can the church meet this demand? What kind of curriculum will guide adults in their spiritual development? What kind of education will help them master interpersonal relationships?

As we catch up with the production of economic goods and have more time for leisure, will we be satisfied with a half-hour lecture about religion on Sunday morning? Leisure can be the way to the abundant life. But abundance is not simply quantitative; it is qualitative too. Where shall we learn the values of the good life? Can the church lead adults in discovering it? This may require learning new skills in recreation, in arts and crafts. These require time and leadership.

As persons have time to think, they can ask some of the more purposeful and penetrating questions about life. Ask any preacher, and he will tell you about the questions on religion that he encounters week after week. He has too little time to answer them. Caught in these Sunday-to-Sunday "time traps," he dilutes his replies. He is always under pressure, moreover, to put the gospel truth in terms of secular symbols because the people do not understand the biblical ones. So may the day hasten when people ask questions that require *more* than statistical answers. When they do, the church must be ready.

A few years ago the ministers at Montview Boulevard Presbyterian Church in Denver did a courageous and unexpected thing. They invited any member of the congregation to start a study group on any topic he desired. Persons with real needs took the initiative and called the church office. They were asked to call together five to fifteen persons. The church provided space in which they might meet. In 1953 and 1954 they formed about thirty such adult groups.

These small groups proceeded by talking things over face to face. One group read plays and discussed them, another novels. Another studied "The Unfolding Drama of the Bible."

13

Parents' problems, foreign policy, prayer and worship, religion in the public schools—all attracted others. A group of doctors in the church met to discuss such topics as "What Does a Christian Say About Birth Control?" "Health Insurance," and "Politics in Hospitals."

## The Dynamics of Small Groups

This discovery of the inner dynamics of small study groups can be a real boon to the churches who will seek to explore them. Studies in recent years have released the new potential to be found in small groups. Each group is considered a "field of power." It changes continuously. Like a magnetic field, it emits a changing pattern of influence. In turn, it is influenced by other forces within it. This dynamic quality of groups and of the persons within them calls for a restudy of our educational procedures.

Too much Christian adult education has been conceived in the past as formulating a body of biblical or theological knowledge and then drilling it into the minds of the listeners. As John Locke put it, the mind was a "tabula rasa," a blackboard. The teacher's job was to write on it. This concept is diametrically opposed to the dynamic one which conceives persons to be changing spiritual beings.

If persons are dynamic, then they are already in motion. They are seeking, asking questions, making decisions. The leader is a guide. He helps them discover mature insights into the Christian way of life. "What do you believe?" "Which way do you proceed?"

Can the Christian way of life be learned in an environment of hostility, hatred, and anxiety, or rather in an environment of mutual trust, love, and faith? What kind of environment do you have in the adult groups in your church?

What kind of motivation do leaders in your church provide? Do they simply stir up the people? Do they know how to awaken them to goal-seeking activity? What are the new insights into the inner dynamics of motivation?

Is communication merely speaking? How do you communicate a way of life? Is the gospel able to become a force in the lives of people—changing, guiding, and directing their minds and spirits?

How will you relate yourself to others if you believe that they are spiritual beings? How will you relate yourself to God? How can we help others direct their lives by the spirit of Christ?

What is the role of the group in helping adults to become stabilized in their Christian commitments? What disciplines will help persons learn how to change? What changes do adults face as they become mature Christians?

Here are some of the issues that we face in the new era of Christian adult education. This book addresses itself to them. It is an exposition of the dynamics of Christian learning for adults. It is the product of multiple experiences in working with adult groups. The point of view is dynamic, developmental, and personally Christian.

This point of view was accurately summarized by Paul Maves when he wrote:

Education is creative inter-action between persons in which the needs of each are served and in which the experiences of the more mature are available as a resource for the less mature. The old equation of precept and example overlooks the primary factor in education, which is relationship. Thus, in religious education we not only witness to what the grace of God has done, and testify to what it can do, but we also mediate the grace of God in our relationship to those whom we teach.[1]

## Some Needed Changes

The dynamic point of view requires some basic changes in the way we regard people, in how we work with them, and in our procedures in groups. It calls for a sharpening of our perceptions so that members and leaders of groups see and understand what is taking place within those groups. It calls for learning the language of relationships. It calls for a new sensitivity to persons as spiritual beings.

Perhaps the first change calls for a new look at persons. If they are dynamic spiritual beings, they are changing. The task of the leader is not to manipulate them to his preconceived ends; his task is to guide them in discovering for themselves the Christian way of life.

Second. Our adult groups, if they are going to be Christian, must become fellowships of love and understanding. The Christian way of life cannot be learned in a group that is controlled by anxiety, fear, distrust, or hatred.

Third. People change as they participate. If they are forced to remain inactive, they do not change. In any study activity the members need to bring information, share ideas, ask questions, and suggest new plans. No one person can do this for them. Through this process of searching they learn how to relate themselves to others in an attitude of mutual trust, and to God, whose nature is love.

[1] "Implications of the Findings of the Sciences of Man," *Religious Education*, XLVI (Sept.-Oct., 1951), 273.

Fourth. Members of the group must learn some new disciplines. These disciplines will not be imposed from without by some authority; they will be self-disciplines. They will be attempts at self-control by persons who would allow the spirit of Christ a chance to work in the group. They will be disciplines that seek to help people who are trying to find their way through the confusions of the propaganda of our time into the biblical truth. These disciplines will restrain a person from telling all the answers. Rather, they will help him encourage his fellow seeker to discover the answer for himself. Thus his knowledge will be a personal knowledge of a spiritual reality.

Fifth. This kind of learning involves the recognition and treatment of others as persons. It is more than the mastering of simple biblical or complex theological ideas. It involves a living relationship between man and God, between man and man, and between man and the deep recesses of his own soul. These relationships have a quality different from the skills that a person brings to things he uses. As he learns to regard himself as a child of God, to relate himself to others as persons who have integrity, a wholesomeness of being, he can relate himself to God in a dynamic, spiritual way.

This is person-to-person learning, the kind of learning that went on between Jesus and his disciples when they learned to recognize him as God incarnate. They knew all the words about God. They had been told them by great lawgivers and prophets, but they learned to know God in a personal way. It was a human, vital, living relationship. We need to change so that this relationship can become a powerful spiritual force in our lives.

Sixth. We need to place more reliance on the Holy Spirit.

Instead of squeezing every lesson into some neat little formula that we intend to superimpose on the adults next Sunday, we need to proceed in a way that will give God a chance. We still have his Spirit in the world. It is still the Christian Era. Let's bring our problems, tensions, decisions, and resolutions to the classroom and give the spirit of Christ a chance to guide us as we think and pray together.

Seventh. The adult group in the church school needs to become a laboratory in which we test the power to create the good and to redeem human life. The sinner, the alcoholic, and the condemned need the healing power of a redemptive Christian group to help them become whole again. This we must try to do. If we fail, let it be in the trying, not because we ignored our Christian obligation.

## A New Era: A New Task

These changes are essential if Christian adult education is to carry out its mission in the new era which is being ushered in by atomic power and automation. This new era demands more of a person than gadgeteering skill. It requires the ability to think, good judgment, a trained imagination, and initiative that is self-imposed.

These qualities of life are basically spiritual. You cannot legislate them. You cannot manipulate people into them. You cannot condition people to them. Those processes were for the materialistic era that is passing.

As we move into the new era where machines will be used more and more to run machines, persons must learn how to live as persons and to relate themselves to God and to other persons. This new development in human relations is a spiritual task. No mechanistic or materialistic approach will suffice.

The church is summoned to the task of developing men and women to their full maturity as spiritual beings.

No era in human history has been filled with so much possibility. The American people can become the best-informed, the best-educated people on earth. Whether or not we plan the kind of educational experiences that meet this situation adequately will depend upon our understanding and application of the dynamics of Christian adult education.

## PROJECTS FOR STUDY AND ACTION

1. List the adult education agencies in your community. What opportunities do they provide?
2. List some of the unmet educational needs of adults in your community.
3. Study about three selected churches in your community. What adult educational needs are they meeting? What needs are they not meeting?
4. If churches were going to provide more adequate programs of adult education, what groups would they start? What studies and activities would they offer?

### BIBLIOGRAPHY

1. *Adult Leadership Magazine.* Mt. Morris, Ill.: Adult Education Association of the U.S.A. Reports on trends and agencies in adult education in the U.S.A. The workshop section contains practical suggestions and procedures.
2. Donahue, Wilma T. *Education for Later Maturity.* New York: Whiteside, Inc., 1955. An excellent introduction into the problems and procedures in working with older adults.
3. Essert, Paul L. *Creative Leadership of Adult Education.* New

York: Prentice-Hall, Inc., 1954. An analysis of basic principles involved in developing leaders for adult education in America.

4. Havighurst, R. J. *Human Development and Education.* New York: Longmans, Green, & Co., 1953. Insightful descriptions of the developmental tasks faced by individuals. The latter part of the book describes the tasks of young adulthood, the middle years, and older adulthood.

5. Howe, Reuel L. *Man's Need and God's Action.* Greenwich, Conn.: Seabury Press, 1953. A theological treatment of the relation of God's grace to man's spiritual need.

6. Kempfer, Homer. *Adult Education.* New York: McGraw-Hill Book Co., 1955. A book for administrators of adult education agencies. It describes principles of program development, organization, and administration.

7. Knowles, Malcolm S. *Informal Adult Education.* New York: Association Press, 1951. A basic introduction to the informal procedures in adult education. Latter part of the book describes types of adult education activities in the Y.M.C.A.

8. Munro, H. C. *Protestant Nurture.* Englewood Cliffs, N.J.: Prentice-Hall, Inc., 1956. A survey of trends in Protestant Christian education in America by a former leader in Christian adult education.

9. Powell, J. W. *Learning Comes of Age.* New York: Association Press, 1956. A survey of the trends and agencies at work in adult education today. Citizenship, family life, job relations, enrichment for living, self-understanding, are included.

10. Sherrill, L. J. *The Gift of Power.* New York: The Macmillan Co., 1955. A definitive portrayal of Christian education that gives primacy to the doctrine of the Holy Spirit. A good treatment of the use of sign and symbol in communication.

# CHAPTER II

# Are Adults Dynamic or Static?

WHAT DO YOU BELIEVE ABOUT ADULTS? DO YOU BELIEVE
they are dynamic or static? Do you believe they are in motion
and changing, or do you believe they need to be stirred up
all the time? Do you believe they have the capacity for self-
direction, or do you believe it is necessary to formulate the
goals for the group and then see to it that they go in that
direction?

## Two Distinct Alternatives

The way you answer these questions will determine the
way you work with a group. If you believe that people are
static, you will have to stir them up and keep after them. You
will keep them moving toward some preconceived goal. If
you believe that they are dynamic—in motion, changing,
capable of self-determination—then you will act as guide,
clarifying alternatives, presenting new information, helping
people establish the right kind of relationships so that they
may keep searching and discovering truth for themselves.

If you believe that adults are static, you probably believe it
is the task of Christian adult education to formulate a fixed
Christian ideology and through the use of group pressures to
squeeze all adults into this mold. If you believe they are
dynamic, the task of Christian adult education becomes an
adventure, a lure, a search, a chance to grow in wisdom and

in favor with God and man. There will be periods of life that are marked by tentativeness and trust. There will also be periods of insight and achievement. Always the search will lure you to study the Bible more thoroughly, to read the works of great religious leaders of the ages, to share your thoughts with others, to try out new spiritual and ethical insights, and to learn more about God and his ways of dealing with men. Do we dare to try it? What is the alternative?

In his arresting book *The Human Use of Human Beings*, Norbert Wiener points out that physicists are capable of making machines that can compute with numbers and can give "yes" and "no" answers to problems involving analogies. Moreover, they can memorize through taping. Using a process called a "feed back" of the material recorded on the tape, the machine can change and correct its answers. These responses are made possible because of the structure of the machine.

"Cybernetics takes the view that the structure of the machine or of the organism is an index of the performance that may be expected from it," asserts Wiener.[1] Thus the hard shell of an insect limits the development of its nervous system. This is the reason that the research scientists in the field of cybernetics and automation work so hard on the control factor in the machine. This control factor regulates its operation. The problem is not in transmitting a quantity of ideas to the machine; it is in the amount the machine can store away and use for action.

Although Wiener would not assert that the machines "learn" to do these functions, his description of their operation comes

[1] (2nd ed.; Garden City, N. Y.: Doubleday & Co., 1954), p. 57. Used by permission of Houghton Mifflin Co.

close to Pavlov's conditioned reflex theory of learning. This theory is built upon the idea that the person or object is static by virtue of its structure. All that the controlling mind has to do to get a predetermined response is to feed in the data.

Does very much of our adult education in the churches go beyond this mechanistic process? Are we educating our people to become victims of this kind of standardization? What are the implications of this procedure if we continue it without a reappraisal of our basic presuppositions?

## Mass Media and the Robot Mind

We live in an age of mass communication. If the creators of the machines are nurtured and schooled on the theory of the "conditioned reflex," will it also determine the process and the content of what is communicated? Will the fixed structure of the mass media tend to standardize the thought patterns of the programs produced?

Wiener seems to be alarmed about the thinness of the current stream of thought coming over the airways, and when he looks at the schools producing the communicators for tomorrow, he warns:

What sometimes enrages me . . . is the preference of great schools of learning for the derivative as opposed to the original; for the conventional and thin, which can be duplicated in many copies, rather than the new and powerful; and for arid correctness and limitation of scope and method, rather than for universal newness and beauty . . . . the axe which has been put to the root of originality because the people who have elected communication as a carrier so often have nothing more to communicate.[2]

[2] *Ibid.*, p. 135.

The adults whose minds are filled with this stream of communications will be attending our churches on Sunday. How shall we work with them? Shall we work on the theory that the teacher has a predigested knowledge of biblical facts, which it is the duty of the adults to absorb? Or shall we proceed on the basis that adults can think, discover insights, and change their way of living if they are guided in a study of the Bible, rather than if they are told the answers? Shall we proceed upon the assumption that adult learning is a stock pile of biblical facts and theological definitions that we add to what the person has already accumulated? Or shall we assert that all learning depends upon the process by which the adult changes as he assimilates new ideas and experiences, as his spiritual needs are illumined, his awareness sensitized, his understanding deepened, his will strengthened, and his decisions reinforced by the Christian group?

## "Go Back to School"

Recently the commercial world was startled by the edict of a top executive in the Bell Telephone Company of Philadelphia. He called his subordinates together and asked them to go back to school. Were they to take more scientific courses in communications? No; they were to take liberal arts courses in literature, philosophy, ethics. Why? This executive was tired of having people around him who knew all the right answers to unimportant questions. He wanted to consult with persons who could ask basic questions about life.

Does the church dare to pursue its educational task as if men and women were dynamic and developing spiritual beings in search of the meaning of life? Or must it treat them as static beings who are merely able to recite right answers to

24

predetermined theological questions and biblical interpretations? As the age of mass communication advances, the pressures will be on the churches to follow the pattern of "Tell them" and "Stamp the teachings into their minds." Many will yield to it, following the path of least resistance.

Christian adult education would be quite simple if we merely had to stimulate the sensory nerves with a Bible verse and, presto, this would be propelled along a neuron until we observed the response of Christian conduct. But alas, the "stimulus-response" bond theory of learning is an inadequate basis for teaching Christianity. Learning the Christian way of life is considerably more dynamic and personal.

Have you ever watched a child learn to eat? It may take him a year to learn to get a spoonful of soup from a bowl to his mouth with any great amount of skill. Why? K. S. Lashley, a psychologist, observed that the child in this situation is at the threshold which affords many options. The stimulus and response are merely mutual fields of power that attract each other. Within these fields there is room for much spontaneous activity. Many pathways lie open over which the power in each field may travel. The control factors are on the one hand the interests, the things the ego wants, the sense of power; and on the other hand the social demands of the group of which he is a part.

Any approach to adult education must present all of these factors—interests, values, social demands—if we seek to guide persons in becoming mature Christians. If we dare to believe that men and women are free moral agents who can live by a spirit, we will affirm that God who is spirit will seek to impart his spiritual power to them. We will dare to believe that God is seeking to reveal his will to men and that they can discern it for themselves. We will dare to believe that men and women who are sensitive to the spiritual influences of other Christians can change under their own self-direction from selfishness to service, from fear to trust in God, from hatred to love toward others.

## Adults Are Dynamic

The dynamic approach to Christian adult education asserts that every adult is a dynamic field of spiritual power, sensitive to spiritual influences. It dares to believe that each person can change under his own self-control when he discovers his relatedness to God and to his fellow men.

"All real living is meeting," says Martin Buber. "No system of ideas, no foreknowledge, and no fancy intervene between I and thou. . . . In the face of the directness of the relation, everything indirect becomes irrelevant." [3]

This dynamic theory of learning acknowledges the relatedness of the universe and of man to God and of man to man. This relatedness is not based on fixed, static, materialistic objects which control what is to be learned and how much can be learned, but on the dynamic view of the universe as a spiritual force and of man as a spiritual being in motion. When this relatedness is perceived and understood, persons do not relate themselves to God as an *object* nor to their fellow men as *things*. The establishment of a personal relationship is basic in dynamic Christian adult education.

This theory dares to affirm that when persons change they feel a new source of spiritual energy released within them. This may be in the form of inner illumination when one discovers his personal relation to God. It may be in the form of

[3] *I and Thou* (New York: Chas. Scribner's Sons, 1937), pp. 11-12.

quickening power when he makes a moral resolve. It may be in a response of trust to persons when he becomes aware that he is a channel for the love of God. It can flow through him and affect the lives of other persons. He can become related to persons as sons of God.

This theory dares to believe that an adult group in the church school can become a field of spiritual power. Through the sharing of religious experiences persons gain insights and learn new meanings. As they relate these symbols to their own experiences, they can change. As persons become involved in the activities of the group, they can discern their own abilities and shortcomings, their need for dependence on God, as well as the need to change. These experiences become the matrix of growth.

This theory contends that every adult not only has the power to learn but has different needs, different tensions, different creative abilities, and different spiritual insights. Moreover, these powers can be developed best in a Christian fellowship. In fact, we have serious doubt as to whether these powers can develop if there is hostility or hatred within the group. We think that when a person is blocked by having others give him all the answers, he will become hostile and overaggressive. He must have the opportunity to work out the implications of the Christian way of life as he assumes the role of a Christian in many life situations.

This theory holds that the interpersonal relations in an adult group set up a field of power in which the individual will be spurred on to reformulate his thoughts, to change his ways of acting, and to acquire new spiritual insights even when he may be arrested in his development. If he feels accepted, he will try to think new thoughts and will try new ways of living. If

27

he feels rejected, his efforts will be seriously curtailed and his development stopped. The interpersonal relations in a Christian group are pivotal.

If we expect adults to climb up the ladder of maturity from a religion of ethical rules to conceptualized theology and on to the life of the Christian spirit, then we need to work with them in ways that will assist dynamic spiritual development.

## PROJECTS FOR STUDY AND ACTION

1. Attend an adult class in the church school. Did the leaders work with the members as if they were dynamic or static? Describe procedures illustrating your answer.

2. Listen to four radio or television programs that you think are educational. Do they help to prepare you to think or do they tell you what to think?

3. Contrast the conditioned reflex theory of learning with dynamic development. What are the essential differences?

4. Visit two classes in a church school, one in which the leader teaches by "stamping it in" and the other in which the leader helps persons to use the biblical material and to think for themselves. Compare the attitudes toward the class of three persons in each class.

5. Try to think of something you have learned recently. Write out a brief description of how you learned it. Compare this learning process with the one you observed in your adult class last Sunday.

### BIBLIOGRAPHY

1. Cantor, Nathaniel. *The Dynamics of Learning*. Buffalo, N.Y.: Foster & Stewart, Inc., 1946. A description of a dynamic learning

theory containing much illustrative material developed in working with teachers.

2. Gleason, George. *Single Young Adults in the Church*. New York: Association Press, 1952. A survey of 222 churches in the West. It describes what single young adults seek to find in the church and then gives a description of the programs they find.

3. Hiltner, Seward. *Self-Understanding*. New York: Chas. Scribner's Sons, 1951. An excellent treatment of some basic psychological concepts such as emotions, perception, growth, and so on. It is documented with biblical case histories.

4. *Man and His Years*. Raleigh, N.C.: Health Publications Institute, Inc., 1950. Sponsored by Federal Security Agency. Conference reports on the problems of aging by some of the best thinkers in this field of study.

5. Maves, Paul B. *The Best Is Yet to Be*. Philadelphia: Westminster Press, 1951. An analysis of the developmental tasks of older adulthood, written from a religious educator's point of view. Practical and perceptive.

6. May, Rollo. *Man's Search for Himself*. New York: W. W. Norton & Co., 1953. Contains clear perceptions of the problems and pressures on modern man.

7. Murphy, Gardner. *Personality*. New York: Harper & Bros., 1947. A biosocial treatment of the processes by which personality develops. For advanced students.

8. Overstreet, H. A. *The Mature Mind*. New York: W. W. Norton & Co., 1949. A definitive description of maturing. Contains philosophical as well as psychological insights.

9. Stieglitz, Edward J. *The Second Forty Years*. Philadelphia: J. B. Lippincott, Co., 1946. A description of the physiological and psychological forces involved in later maturity.

10. Wiener, Norbert. *The Human Use of Human Beings*. 2nd ed. New York: Doubleday & Co., 1954. The implications of automation for setting men free to develop as persons.

# CHAPTER III

# The Dynamics of Participation

GROUPS ARE ESSENTIAL IN HELPING ADULTS EXPLORE THE Christian way of life. In a group each member expresses himself so that he may be understood. He awakens new ideas in minds of others. During this interplay of ideas many opinions are modified. Through these interpersonal relationships people change their attitudes and their ways of behaving.

## "You Can't Be Christian Alone"

This approach to our educational task is not new. Jesus Christ picked a group of disciples. He lived with them, taught them. He brought them through these experiences into a living, vital fellowship. This fellowship was broken by his death. It had been such a powerful force in the lives of his followers, however, that they could not abandon it. The disciples, although scattered by the tragic incidents that culminated in his death, reassembled to carry on the fellowship, in spite of threats and persecutions. When they came together, there was a spiritual quickening. The guiding image of Christ was still present with real power and influence within their lives. The persons who belonged to the fellowship experienced a new motivation which they did not have as separate, unrelated individuals. The biblical record states that "they devoted themselves to the apostles' teaching and fellowship, to the breaking of bread and the prayers" (Acts 2:42 R.S.V.).

## Dynamic Forces in a Group

In recent years the students of group dynamics have rediscovered the field of forces that operates within a group. They realize that a group is more than the sum total of the persons who belong in it. As each person influences the others, there is an interplay of stimuli among them.

Within this "field," members are always thrusting energy and receiving energy. They are interrelated. As Wesner Fallaw points out,

The group, as the field within which growth and learning are made possible, does not constitute a situation in which learning takes place as simple stimulus-response or mechanistic conditioning. Within the group the arrows of attraction (stimuli) point both to and from individuals—some persons having more, some less than others—weaving back and forth and crosswise, making a pattern, a configuration. Persons are responding to each other and to the stimulus of the group as a whole. The influence of the group transcends the combined influences of all the persons in it.[1]

Within the group each person finds either acceptance or rejection. Through the expression of ideas and through his influence, which is received and understood, he gains clarity of insight and a deeper understanding of himself. When a person is rejected and forced to live in isolation, he begins to react against the group. Rejection causes some people to become defensive, to withdraw, to remain hidden because they have been hurt. This does not bring maximum growth and

[1] "The Function of Groups in Learning Christianity," *Religious Education,* November-December, 1950, pp. 323-24. Used by permission.

development of a person. Quite frequently it brings about a blighted life and engenders a social problem. Rejection causes some persons to withdraw for a while; later they may attack the group. If the group will not accept them, they may propose to destroy it. In this way they become a source of social irritation.

It is all-important that people find a real sense of belonging in a Christian group. They must feel the warmth of the fellowship and the worth of their own participation in it. Simple attendance at meetings is not participation. A crowded and exhaustive schedule of meetings may help to fatigue adults and thereby release tensions, but it does not change their spirits. The real participation that we seek involves the basic intentionality of the whole person. Some psychologists refer to this as "ego-involvement." G. W. Allport states:

In insisting that participation depends upon ego-involvement, it would be a mistake if we were to assume that we are dealing with a wholly self-centered and parasitic ego that demands unlimited status and power for the individual himself. Often, indeed, the ego is clamorous, jealous, possessive and cantankerous. But this is true chiefly when it is forced to be *reactive* against constant threats and deprivations. We all know of "power-people" who cannot, as we say, "submerge their egos." The trouble comes, I suspect, not because their egos are unsubmerged, but because they are still reactive toward some outer or inner features of the situation which are causing conflicts and insecurity. Reactive egos tend to perceive their neighbors and associates as threats rather than as collaborators. . . .

Participation, as opposed to peripheral motor activity, sinks a shaft into the inner-subjective regions of the personality. It taps central values. Thus in studying participation the psychologist has an approach to the complete person.[2]

## Participation: Authority-Centered or Interactive?

Since there are many degrees of participation in any learning group, it may be revealing to appraise the amount of freedom or control within a group with a view to discovering its effect upon participation. In their experiments with group climate, Kurt Lewin and Ronald Lippitt found that autocratic groups had a much higher tension level than democratic groups or uncontrolled *laissez faire* groups. The leadership in autocratic groups kept the members under very strict control at all times. The leaders were rigid and demanded unquestioning obedience to their commands. In spite of the appearance of quietness and order in an autocratic group, however, there was a high degree of inattention.

Since an autocratic atmosphere is less permissive than a democratic one . . . we may wonder how a higher level of inter-group aggression can occur in an autocracy. The answer lies in the fact that the restrictive character of autocracy has two contradictory effects: (a) it leads to frustration of the group and therefore to an increase of aggression, and (b) the control aspect of restriction is equivalent to a restricting force again and it increases group aggression. This inner contradiction is inherent in every autocratic situation and is the basis of a high tension level.[3]

This knowledge of the effects of autocratic group leadership

[2] "The Psychology of Participation," *The Psychological Review,* LII (May, 1945), 123, 130. Used by permission of the publisher.

[3] Kurt, Lewin, "Frontiers in Group Dynamics," *Human Relations,* (Ann Arbor, Michigan: Research Center for Group Dynamics, 1947-48), I, 20-21.

should have a profound effect on the way we work with groups in the church.

One summer I observed as a participant member both an authoritarian-led class and a dynamic Christian fellowship at work. In the traditional and formal class the professor lectured throughout and tested the students every week. His educational procedure was a conscious attempt to stamp certain ideas into the minds of the students. At the end of the summer term the tension among and within the members was terrific. The final exams were slammed on the desks as students stalked out. One person said, "I'm going on a binge. I want to forget the whole affair."

Later that summer I shared as a participant-observer in a fellowship of Christians. By sharing experiences they learned from one another. They developed appreciations and insights that helped one another. At the end of these experiences, the members of the group had developed such a quality of interrelatedness that they stayed and talked together at length after the classes were over. Moreover, they compiled a list of names and addresses of all members. They wanted to write to one another and continue the fellowship.

In a truly Christian group the level of tension between persons is not heightened to the breaking point. Although there may be conflicts among persons who disagree vigorously, these conflicts are clarified through interaction.

There is a real need for Christian groups to determine whether they will be the kind of fellowship in which persons grow toward maturity and understanding through interaction and clarification, or whether they will become authoritarian-led groups which reject all persons who are not orthodox in their beliefs. They must decide whether a leader will work out a preconceived program and then seek to put it across by turning on the pressure to get the folks to do, or whether they will work out objectives together and make plans to achieve them.

## The Christian Quality of Interaction

Within a Christian fellowship which seeks to help individuals mature, there is need for a climate of acceptance and understanding. The group's faith in one another constitutes a field of power which is conducive to Christian growth. In a group where anxieties are heightened continuously, faith has little chance to grow. Fear destroys faith. Moreover, in a Christian group that seeks to relate persons to a God of love, the members need to operate so that they reveal that love at work in their own lives.

When adults who belong to a Christian group discuss a question, they communicate more than ideas. Of course, ideas must be stated clearly so that other persons in the group will understand what is being said. However, persons also communicate something of themselves, their attitudes, their desires, the feelings, and their hopes. Understanding is more than perception with clarity of the words one says. It is based on insights concerning the personality of the other individual. Words are peripheral responses. Feelings, sentiments, hopes, are expressions of a deeper personal "region." Real participation in a group, therefore, involves the ability to understand these inner responses of the other persons, as well as the ideas which they speak.

In any Christian group that seeks to discover truth, there must be an element of mutual trust. Each person thinks of the

35

other as a disciple or a fellow seeker. According to Ross Snyder, of the University of Chicago:

Our picture and our feelings about others color everything that we say or do. Knowing this to be true also of others, we have all learned to watch what is going on so that we may catch the guiding image which other people have of us. We are more free to create when we feel that their guiding image is one which sees us as a person who is trying to discover the truth. With this perception from others of ourselves, we find ourselves able to contribute more deeply and more truly. We find it possible also to be more productive. (All creation seems to depend upon a climate of approval!)

If, on the other hand, we get from each other a negative report in regard to this guiding image, then we commence to defend ourselves. We become extremely busy on the inside, carrying on a dialogue which reiterates that after all we are worthy and we are now being mistreated. This inner conflict can be so disturbing that we have no time left to be productive. We may become those members of the group who live a disagreeable life of subtle but ugly protest.[4]

Perhaps the most difficult factor with which to cope in guiding or participating in a discussion group is the fact that the inner personal region of any member may be threatened. When he feels he is not accepted, or when the field force of the group seems to set a dynamic force in action against him, the inner personal region of that member begins to explode. Either persons participate or they tend to withdraw and react against the group.

This psychological effect is tremendously important if the

[4] "Necessary Processes in a Productive Group" (Unpublished paper), pp. 4-5.

group is to have a redemptive influence or a healing effect upon the lives of other persons in the group. Through this process either the redeeming love of God is at work in the lives of people or it is short-circuited by opinionated selfishness. There is always a danger in Christian groups that someone will use the threat of biblical orthodoxy or moralistic values to cudgel people into conformity. As this kind of coercion is used, members of the group begin to return peripheral responses and move away from the responses of the inner personal region.

If a person feels that he is understood as a self, even though others disagree with his ideas, he still has acceptance in the group. He can live with them. He can still belong. The channel is open whereby he can communicate. There remains the possibility that the spiritual values of redeeming love can do their work in the lives of members. If a person is accepted by the group, he can accept the grace of God and begin to change.

It was something of this same idea that I had in mind when I wrote:

Most of the adults who attend a class do so of their own free will and accord. They have been fighting against fatigue and the routine of work. Many of them may be fighting against physical breakdowns due to aging or disease. They need the sustaining power this fellowship of Christians can give them. They are people with feelings. They are capable of becoming better people than they now are. Jesus never doubted that the redeeming love of God would help them. He worked to help them discover it for their own lives.

We need to remember that no matter what a person says on Sunday morning, it really makes sense to him and to his whole

37

way of life. His statement may be a compensation for bafflement. In the very act of uttering it he may see his own confusion and begin to clarify his thoughts.

If we would study the relationship between Jesus and his disciples, I think we would soon conclude that these followers of his were very ordinary people. Yet Jesus never doubted the possibility of what they might become if the power of God could get hold of their lives. Moreover, he knew that the power of God had a greater chance within the fellowship of disciples than it would have if the disciples had not been brought together into a loving fellowship.[5]

## Levels of Participation

A church group that takes into account the worth of persons and their need to belong, to clarify ethical values, to be redeemed, and to change under the power of the spirit of Christ, will be aware of the deeper levels of participation that are necessary. At one level the persons may be speaking ideas merely for their own clarification or to see what effect they will have on the others. There is another level at which persons speak ideas and feel that they are understood. They know that others trust them. When members of a group attain this degree of maturity, they are not troubled when other people reject their ideas. They know others do not reject them as persons. A group needs to develop this quality of interrelatedness before it can do much to change the quality of the lives of its members.

At the first level of participation there is little togetherness, because persons within the group do not clearly understand the ideas put forth by the other persons. Every person is seeking for a place in the group. During this period one may get

[5] "Is It Really Christian Education?" *Adult Student,* April, 1951, p. 11.

reactions from some members of the group, indicating that the group is wasting time or suggesting that they would like to do something "more active." Later, these persons may help the group initiate some action.

Or one may hear the plea, "I'm so confused; why don't you tell us the answers?" These persons are seeking information; telling them the answers would stop the search. Each person needs to see the other person in the role that he assumes as a part of the group. Later he may observe that person change both ideas and roles.

During the second stage of development there is conflict between ideas. Participation increases. Rejection of the opinion of others and even frustration about one's own convictions may emerge. The differences of opinions between members become sharper. The clash of opinions may lead to a greater clarity of ideas or to individual frustration. Through this process the group begins to discover the real issues.

While conflict and clarification of ideas go on, the leader may receive a considerable amount of criticism. He needs to understand that much of this criticism may not be directed at him as a leader but that the fact that he is in a position of leadership makes him the target toward which a person who cannot formulate his own convictions may direct his inner tensions. He may project his frustration momentarily onto the leader.

At this moment it is necessary that the leader be a good listener. After a member expresses his ideas, he may say to himself, "What have I said? Is it really true? Do I need to rethink it?" Through this process he may discover a new way of stating his beliefs that he has not previously conceived. This same process may take place between any two or three individuals. They may discover that leadership is not the function of one person. It is distributed among all members of the group as they seek to lead one another out in their thinking. Perhaps the most difficult problem faced by members of the group at this point is how to ask the right questions, the questions that will start people rethinking their own opinions in the light of new facts and new values, and that will help them gain an insight into the problems which they face.

The third phase may be best described as a time when many of the differences are reconciled. Persons settle down to the task of working together to find solutions to their problems. Disagreement is usually at a minimum. At least there is a basic trust in the guiding image of the other person. Although the members may differ about ideas and notions, flat rejection of a proposal is seldom spoken. Usually persons are saying, "Now couldn't we say that another way?" Or, "Is this what you mean?"

During this phase of the development, the persons who try to reconcile different opinions may take the leadership within the group. The chairman seeks to give them a great deal of freedom and does not project his own opinion into the group too much. They are beginning to develop a cohesivensss. He wants to aid this development by not having the group depend upon him for decisions and direction. He may ask persons to summarize from time to time. He may try to bring out a response from some of the "quiet ones." He may want to see how far these persons have come in their thinking. He may want to see how much they are accepting or rejecting the new centers of thought which the group has discovered.

There is one real danger in this process, however. If the group stays at this level too long, it may become very complacent about its own conclusions and fail to move on to a group decision and action.

In the fourth phase of development, the members of the group retain the kind of cohesiveness which they achieved in the third phase, but they now begin to work definite plans of action. They develop a sense of urgency and become effective individuals who work well with others in the group.

It is here that the Christian concepts of mission and vocation may take on real meaning and significance in the lives of these persons. Here is where the fellowship may be subdivided into small groups that work on some problem-solving activity which would change the community. Or here is where individuals take up their responsibilities outside of this group and try to work toward solutions as far as they have influence or responsibility. These persons still use the group as a base for security, inspiration, and the clarification of ideas.

Understanding the patterns and the levels of participation is essential if Christian groups are going to complete their "task-oriented" and "person-oriented" functions. Leaders need to assist this process of interaction. Members need to develop attitudes toward others and to control through self-discipline the ways in which they relate themselves to others, so that their participation is based on real understandings of the group process in which they are involved and on the spiritual needs of persons to whom they are related.

## PROJECTS FOR STUDY AND ACTION

1. How would you rate the following assemblages of individuals from the standpoint of group cohesiveness? Why?

   a) A crowd at the scene of an accident
   b) Boys around a street light
   c) A church school class on Sunday
   d) A crowd at a ball game
   e) Delegates to a conference
   f) A football team
   g) A Parent Teacher Association meeting
   h) A labor union

2. Talk with someone who has been rejected from some group and discover how he feels "on the inside." As you listen to him, compare his feelings with your own.

3. Observe a group in the church. What factors were helping; what factors were hindering the group in solving its problems? How could the group improve its ways of operating?

4. Observe a discussion group, and chart the levels of participation. Note the amount of time it takes to move from one level to another.

5. Visit a church-school class. Tabulate the number of times persons seek to help others; indicate they understand what the other person says; delegate authority to others; express trust. Tabulate also the number of times they speak to defend their own positions; dictate to others what they should do; make snap judgments without facts or information.

## BIBLIOGRAPHY

1. Allport, G. W. "The Psychology of Participation," *The Psychological Review*, LII (May, 1945), 117-32. An excellent article on acceptance and rejection in groups.

2. Douty, M. A. *How to Work with Church Groups*. Nashville,

Tenn.: Abingdon Press, 1957. An introduction to the ways of working with groups in the church.

3. Kubie, Susan H., and Landau, Gertrude. *Group Work with the Aged.* New York: International Universities Press, 1953. Encouraging ways of increasing older adult co-operation in group activities.

4. Lippitt, G. L. "Religious Education and Group Dynamics," *Religious Education,* XLVII (November-December, 1952), 372-77. An article summarizing the preparation needed and the basic steps involved in leading a group.

5. Lowry, Louis. *Adult Education and Group Work.* New York: William Morrow & Co., 1955. Principles of group work in liberal adult education, with specific help in young adult, parent, and older adult education.

6. Murray, Janet P. and Clyde E. *Guide Lines for Group Leaders.* New York: Whiteside, Inc., 1954. Suggestions to leaders in working democratically with groups.

7. Newcomb, Theodore M. *Social Psychology.* New York: Dryden Press, 1950. A survey of current insights and trends in social psychology. Advanced reading.

8. Schmidt, W. H., and Buchanan, P. C. *Techniques That Produce Teamwork.* New York: Appleton-Century-Crofts, 1954. A discussion of ways to encourage staff action and freedom of expression.

9. Snyder, Ross, *et al.* "Group Dynamics and Religious Education," *Religious Education,* XLVI (November-December, 1951), 323-44. A simple introduction to the use of group dynamics in religious education.

10. Thelen, H. A. *Dynamics of Groups at Work.* Chicago: University of Chicago Press, 1954. A description of basic principles of changes that occur in groups. Good suggestions for improving meetings, ways persons may participate, evaluating, and group operation. Advanced reading.

11. Trecker, Audrey and Harleigh. *How to Work with Groups.* New York: Woman's Press, 1952. A practical guide to conducting a meeting, leading a discussion, working with a committee, publicity, financing, and leadership.

12. *Understanding How Groups Work* (pamphlet). Adult Education Association, 1955. A pamphlet containing a series of articles on diagnosing group problems such as apathy, indecision, conflict, pressures, etc.

# CHAPTER IV

# A Little Motivation Goes a Long Way

ONE DAY WHILE TRAVELING BY TRAIN I ASKED THE GENTLE-
man who shared the coach seat with me, "What do you do
for a living?"

He replied, "I train clerks for a big department store in
Pittsburgh."

"Is that so?" I responded with a look of pleasant surprise.
"I am engaged in adult education too. I suppose that you tell
them all about the principles of good salesmanship and then
give them a lecture on the history of the store."

"I haven't given a lecture in ten years," he retorted.

"Well, how do you do it?" I inquired.

"We begin with a customer who wants to buy a specific
thing, and then we demonstrate how a salesperson would
handle that particular customer," was his answer.

## Motivation Is Related to Interests

Could it be that he had something? Is it better to begin with
a real situation or with some abstract principle? How do you
motivate people to want to learn? Will they really begin to
think when they face a very specific problem and need to
make a decision about it? What do you think?

One of the first jobs of a leader is to discover interest
among the students in the group. The students want something. They may like the folk who are in the group. They

may feel a lack in their lives and have a wistful hope that perhaps a study in a particular field will help them. Many of them resist change. They merely want someone with knowledge to reaffirm the opinionated judgments which they already hold. If learning is going to take place, the leader must discover their real interests and relate his subject matter to those interests. This is the basis of motivation.

While leading a group in a leadership school one summer, I was asked by a teacher of an adult class, "How would you get a group of adults interested in studying about Hannah, the mother of Samuel?" Hannah seems remote. There is very little in common between the families of a primitive pastoral people and families in our city civilization. Whatever was done, I knew we would need to jar the group out of their complacent attitude toward this subject.

I chose two women who were opposites and asked them to discuss Hannah before the class. One of the two was pensive, meditative, mystical; the other was an activist and an extrovert. One was asked to have a favorable attitude toward Hannah, the other a negative one. The conversation went something like this:

"Don't you think it was wonderful for Hannah to give up her son to the church to be trained for religious work?"

"Oh, I don't see anything wonderful about that. I wish some organization would take my kids off my hands. They take up too much of my time."

"But you don't understand. Here was a mother who loved her child, yet she was willing to give him up so that he could develop into a leader of his people."

"I wish our church had a nursery. I would send all three

of my children down there so fast that the attendant would be bowled over as they rushed through the door!"

"Surely you will admit that Hannah made a great sacrifice of her present pleasures in order that her son might develop more than he would have if he had remained at home."

"A clever scheme to get him out from underfoot. It would have been a greater sacrifice if she had kept him at home and trained him herself. Ask any parent here."

In a few minutes these two women had the other members of the class interjecting their points of view. Each member wanted to express his own idea. The subject was no longer remote; it was real. I dealt with the relation of children to parents and families to the church. They found that their own egos were involved in the discussion. All had opinions on the subject and were ready to express them. Their interest had been stirred, and they wanted to participate. In every learning situation a little motivation goes a long way.

Real motivation for adult learning arises out of the desires of people. No matter what the subject or the skill to be learned, the adult asks the question, "Is it relevant?" The leader must help the members of the group discover those ties that relate this bit of knowledge to their needs.

## Role Playing Enlivens a Group

When Kurt Lewin and his associates Alvin Zander and Ronald Lippitt were working on this problem, they came to the conclusion that real life situations should be brought into the classroom wherever possible. The more people talked about a problem without seeing their relationship to it, the less interested they became. They tried to bring real life situations into the classroom and to rehearse them dramatically before the whole group.

"It has become increasingly clear that in only a small portion of our teaching procedures can we be satisfied with the effective transmission of *information*," state Alvin Zander and Ronald Lippitt. "More often the educational obligation is to transmit actual *performance* skills or to create basic *attitudes*." [1] The procedures used to accomplish these purposes were called "role playing."

In role playing a person acts out the way he would respond in a specific situation. There is no script. He responds spontaneously. Naturally he creates the role in terms of his own background, experience, and understanding. This helps the audience understand how such a person thinks and feels in this situation. They can identify many kindred feelings of their own. In this way they are led to greater self-understanding and to a better understanding of others. For example, a person may portray the way an older adult feels when he has been retired from his job after forty years. As persons in the group watch, they gain insights into problems they will face and they gain understandings of what an older adult is facing now. This is motivational. The problem is no longer remote. It is real. It is in the classroom. After such a demonstration, wise leadership can move easily to a discussion of such a question as, "How may our church serve the older adults of this community better?"

In using role playing there are a few simple rules. It is not a cure-all for dull classes. Use it sparingly. We use role playing to introduce problems in interpersonal relations—family sit-

[1] "Reality Practice as Educational Method," *Sociometry*, VII (1944), 130.

uations, associations with persons at work, ethical conflicts—and to create an interest in biblical persons, such as Nicodemus, the Samaritan woman, David and Jonathan, Micaiah and the king, and so on. Start simply with a nonthreatening situation. Ask persons to assume roles that are not theirs in real life. Let persons volunteer for the roles. Explain the situation carefully. If it involves two or more persons, let them get together briefly and work out their own approach. Do not let them rehearse their lines—this curtails spontaneity.

There are many ways of involving the audience. Ask sections to identify with certain persons and then to show how they would handle a situation. Or groups may listen for points with which they agree, others for points with which they disagree, others for issues they want to discuss further. Through this process tensions are released, insights gained, preconceived notions exploded, and persons are ready to think with greater understanding.

## "Complacency Shock" Bans Boredom

Quite frequently we need to move adults from attitudes of complacency to personal involvement so that they may participate in the group. The technique of complacency shock may be used as a means of creating increased interest. It is also a means of overcoming any natural resistance to change.

However, there is a great deal of misunderstanding about the term. It does not mean personal attack. Leland Bradford and Paul Sheats, who have used complacency shock to train teachers in new methods of work, contend that "before effective training can take place, help must be given to potential trainees to enable them to move from clutching the *status quo* to developing an interest in change. Such help, however, must be based on a diagnosis of causes." They suggest the follow-ing analyses:

1. The trainee with a reputation around one form of behavior . . . must be shown that change will improve his position.
2. The trainee with no experience of what could be . . . must be given a picture of the improved results to be expected of the proposed change and a realization that he can be successful in making such a change.
3. The person who sees only one side of an issue . . . must be helped by stretching the perception of the trainee.
4. When there is individual or group insecurity . . . they must be helped to see that through insight and mastery a trainee can accomplish much more in the future.[2]

These are the objectives of the dialogue in complacency shock. Persons are jarred out of their complacency without being destroyed in the spiritual depths of their beings.

It is also clear that much of the resistance to change is due to group inertia. Unless the group is motivated to want to change, its resistance will overcome the desire to change which any individual may express. If the group members face a problem together or accept a new set of values, the indi-viduals in it will strengthen each other in their efforts to overcome their weaknesses. This is the basic principle that makes the work of Alcoholics Anonymous so effective.

*Sociodrama Involves People*

As a means of awakening young adults to the possibilities of more intelligent planning within their groups, the writer

[2] From "Complacency Shock, a Prerequisite to Training," by Leland Bradford and Paul Sheats, contained in *Sociatry*, Vol. II, No. 1, 1948, Editor J. L. Moreno, M.D., published by Beacon House, Inc.

has found the technique of sociodrama to be very useful in training sessions.

Sociodrama is the spontaneous enactment by two or more persons of a conflict situation in interpersonal relations. Differences are pronounced, and alternatives are clarified through these interactions. The members of the audience hear replies to some of their own arguments. They begin to see ways they must change because of the consequences of certain attitudes or ways of behaving which they cherish. Sociodrama may be used to deepen understandings of persons in conflict situations by having persons switch roles. When the argument is at its height, ask the persons involved to change sides and argue from the other point of view. This helps the person who may be under the dominance of a very authoritarian person to feel what happens when he is placed in a more rewarding role. Ask these persons how they felt as they performed each function. The story of Joseph and his brothers lends itself to this approach. It is also useful in approaching problems of intergroup and intercultural conflict. The sociodrama enables persons to enter into the feelings and attitudes of persons and groups in a more perceptive way. When this is done, they are motivated to discuss a problem with a real depth of searching rather than to speak to it "off the top of their minds."

In a young adult conference, for example, some persons indicated a conflict over their proposed use of the church building. A sociodrama was arranged. They selected a committee of three persons and a pastor whom they interviewed to find out whether they could use the church on Wednesday night. He was asked to think of every barrier that might interfere. The young adults were asked to suggest creative activities for their programs.

The conversation went like this:

Minister: "Well, this is really a matter for the Board of Trustees."

Young adult: "But if you are for us, we know they will be more apt to support us."

Minister: "What do you want it for?"

Young adult: "Sunday morning is not enough time to build a really vital fellowship. We could study things more fully if we had more time."

Minister: "If I did this for you, some other groups would want it too. Why, we might have this church in use every night in the week."

Young adult: "Wouldn't it be wonderful if this church could begin to reach two or three times as many people as it is now reaching?"

Minister: "Yes, but I'm not sure that that is the way to do it. What we need is more people who attend the worship service on Sunday."

Young adult: "But if you came to know some of these people personally as they work with you, don't you think they would want to join our church and participate in the Sunday morning worship service?"

Minister: "Well, perhaps, but what would you do if you had the church one night a week? Just have a good time?"

Young adult: "Is there any harm in good wholesome fun at the church? We would have some recreation, parties, hobby nights, learn some crafts, have folk games now and then. We might have a singing group. Jim said he would like to lead a dramatic group; he used to do some of that in school. But that would not be all—"

Minister: "What other activities would you plan?"

Young adult: "We could work on projects for the church too. There are plenty of things around here that need to be done. We thought we might study too. There are a number of good teachers, who are teaching their own classes on Sunday mornings, who could lead us on a week night."

Minister: "Well, I'll think about it. But you don't want me to be a baby sitter for the children, do you?"

Young adult: "No, we are going to let the ladies work out that problem. If they decide to bring the whole family, we'll provide someone for the nursery."

Minister: "Well, if you are willing to go that far in assuming responsibility for this program, I will back you up and see if we can't arrange for you to use the church on Wednesday night."

Young adult: "That's wonderful! I think this church is really going to move ahead under the kind of leadership you are giving us. We certainly are glad we called on you tonight."

Through the use of sociodrama, the reluctant members of the group found that they were caught up in situations which were similar to their own previous experiences. They wanted to participate. They wanted to try out their ideas in this kind of situation. In this way the group becomes a laboratory for trying out one's own approach to a social problem. The individual gains confidence as the group helps him. He changes his way of behaving as he discovers approaches that do not work.

The sociodrama between the minister and the young adult helped to create among the members of the group the desire to change. Many persons began to reassess what they were doing in their own groups in the light of the possibility of using the church during the week. Many of them were asking themselves, "What use will we make of our opportunity to use the church on Wednesday nights?"

The sociodrama focused the attention of the conference upon the problem of providing more enriching experiences for the members if they were going to have a vital experience. It helped break up the complacency pattern of "a class on Sunday morning and a party once a month." It helped them see the possibility of new experiences at other times. It also helped members of the group to diagnose their own problems.

Much of the planning that goes on in young adult groups is done without very much thought being given to the real needs of the members of the group. Often new activities are merely programs that individual members put on without any sense of relating these experiences or activities to the real needs of the group.

After experiencing the sociodrama, members of the class were divided into small groups and were asked to plan some worthwhile experiences for their own groups. Participation in planning activities is a motivating experience also. If a committee does all the work, very little interest will be engendered. In these small planning groups, recorders took down the suggestions as the discussion proceeded. One person recorded eighteen suggestions in twenty minutes, another twenty-two. That is a high rate of productivity. The interest in the groups remained high.

After twenty minutes, the members of the several groups reassembled. The recorders reported the suggestions. These findings were arranged in the following suggested schedule of activities:

53

| | APRIL | MAY | JUNE |
|---|---|---|---|
| *Evangelism* | Visit families with children; invite them to bring children to nursery. Recheck mailing list. Social at church for families that joined church at Easter | Family Night meeting at church to arouse interest of new families. Explain ways church serves families | Pop-in parties for single persons. Invite them to recreational outdoor opportunities |
| *Study and Worship* | *Unit* "Whence Cometh Our Help?" in time of sorrow and suffering | *Unit* "Children Deserve Christian Homes" | *Unit* "Families Make Communities" |
| *Social Action and World Service* | Check on city council about housing project. Have someone from Alcoholics Anonymous speak to the group | Send aid to another country; Korea, India. Help a D.P. family. Have someone from the city government speak to group on law enforcement | Assist in playground supervision. Assist in vacation church school. Volunteer as camp leaders for youth groups |
| *Recreation and Creative Arts* | Sunrise breakfast | Hiking, with a demonstration cookout and campfire | Summer folk festival |

## Goal-seeking Channels Power

The process of setting goals for a group is bound up with the discovery of needs and the planning of activities. When members of a group become involved in planning together, they will raise the question "What is the purpose of this activity?" In seeking an answer to this question, they formulate specific goals and objectives. These goals are formed in the light of the needs of the group and the basic aims of the organization to which they belong.

Motivation is a real outcome of goal-seeking activity. It involves facing and overcoming problems. It involves achievement that brings satisfaction to the person who is seeking these ends.

Great care should be exercised in setting attainable goals for a group. When goals are too idealistic or the problem too overwhelming, persons will lose interest. When goals demand skills or knowledge that is not attainable within the group, members will develop a feeling of frustration and express it with emotional outbursts. When goals are attainable, persons will put forth a great deal of effort to understand new truth and to acquire new skills in order that they may reach the goals.

Parents will put forth a great deal of effort to read books on child psychology or learn skills that relate to the health of their children, because they want to become better parents. Good group leaders will keep the appeal of better parenthood before these persons and encourage their participation in the group activities as a means of attaining it.

Leaders who merely announce that Mrs. Johnston of the Get-Well Baby Clinic will be here to speak next Friday night will not be motivating the listeners very much to come to hear Mrs. Johnston. Motivation comes through goal-seeking activity that meets their needs. They want to become better parents, but they do not particularly care to listen to a lecture. They will listen to a lecture and participate in a forum, however, if they know it will help them attain the goals they seek. Their motivation comes through involvement together in goal-seeking activity.

Through role playing, complacency shock, sociodrama, and goal-seeking activity, adults may be motivated to greater interest and participation in their educational activities. If more time can be spent on motivation and less time in telling them that "they ought to," our groups would be more productive.

Adequate motivation is the vital mainspring of sustained interest that keeps adults learning. If used wisely, a little motivation can go a long way toward keeping adults growing, maturing, and developing as long as they live!

## PROJECTS FOR STUDY AND ACTION

1. Obtain a study unit designated for your church school. Select a lesson. Why would persons want to study this lesson? What appeals would you make to persons who expressed an interest in this lesson?
2. Select a biblical situation and seek to create an interest in discussing it by role playing.
3. Through role playing define the alternatives which a group would discuss concerning family finances. Ask persons in the group to indicate the degree of change in their interest in this subject before and after the role-playing incident.

4. Suppose a leader of your group is perfectly content with the present inadequate program. Through "complacency shock" seek to get him to want to change. Observe carefully the four principles involved in using this technique. Ask a person in the group to observe whether these principles were followed.

5. Through the use of a sociodrama defined very specifically for your situation, seek to involve the whole group in a planning process that will be productive of new ideas. Ask committees to define a worth-while goal and to work out the activities and experiences that would help them reach it.

6. Choose an incident involving some intergroup tension situation. Through sociodrama portray this situation. Ask the group to discuss it.

## BIBLIOGRAPHY

A. *Role Playing*

1. Argyris, Chris. *Role Playing in Action*. Ithaca, N.Y.: New York State School of Industrial and Labor Relations, Cornell University. A booklet describing the use of role playing in improving intergroup relations.

2. Bavelas, Alex. "Role Playing and Management Training," *Sociatry*, I (March, 1947), 183-92. The use of role playing to help persons negotiate face-to-face relationships at work. Step-by-step procedure.

3. Benne, K., Bradford, L., and Lippitt, R. *Group Dynamics and Social Action* (pamphlet). New York: Anti-Defamation League of B'nai B'rith, 1950. Motivating groups to work at problems in intercultural relations.

4. French, John R. P. "Role Playing as a Method of Training Foremen," *Human Factors in Management*. Ed. Schuyler Hoslett. Park College Press, 1946. Use of role playing in training industrial leaders, in solving management-worker relations, and as counselor training.

5. *How to Use Role Playing* (pamphlet). Adult Education Association, 1955, p. 48. A pamphlet describing the procedure to follow in

the use of role playing and giving other tools in the learning process.
6. Klein, Alan F. *Role Playing*. New York: Association Press, 1956. An excellent step-by-step treatment of procedures in the use of role playing.

## B. *Sociodrama and Psychodrama*

1. Bradford, Leland, and Sheats, Paul. "Complacency Shock as a Prerequisite to Training," *Sociatry*, II (1948), 37-49. An article describing the basic principles in the use of complacency shock to motivate people to change.
2. Grambs, Jean D. "Dynamics of Psychodrama in the Teaching Situation." *Sociatry*, I (March, 1948), 383-99. An example of the sensitizing process that overcomes barriers to learning: spontaneity, acceptance, and projection.
3. Jennings, Helen. "Leadership Training through Sociodrama." *National Association of Deans of Women Journal*, X (March, 1947), 112-19. Basic principles in getting leaders to change their ways of working with groups.
4. Moreno, J. L. *Psychodrama and Sociodrama*. New York: Beacon Press, 1946. A definitive work by the pioneer developer of these techniques.
5. Sherif, M., and Cantril, Hadley. *Psychology of Ego-Involvements*. New York: John Wiley & Son, 1947. A very advanced study of factors contributing to ego-involvements. See ch. 10: "Ego Involvement and Identification in Group Situations."

CHAPTER V

# Procedures
# That Increase Participation

IN 1890 ONLY 7 PER CENT OF THE CHILDREN IN THE UNITED
States went to high school. Today the young adults as a group
have completed eleven years of schooling. In 1890 there was
a tremendous need for bringing information to the adult
public. The Chautauqua movement made this one of its
primary aims. It did its job well. It represented one of the
greatest advances in adult education in America.

Today the situation is somewhat different. When adults
come to the church school, they have been bombarded all
week with information *via* the radio, television, newspapers,
and movies. These means of mass communication have poured
an unending stream of opinions and ideas into their heads.
Moreover, adults travel more widely, they talk with more
people, they have many experiences to share. They do not
come empty, waiting to be filled. Rather, they come confused,
overstimulated, wanting to share their ideas with others.

This new situation calls for a more dynamic approach to
adults in our groups in the church school. They are not waiting to be told what to think or do. They want to participate
in a process wherein they can discover their needs, define
their goals, and work out their own way of life together. In a

discussion group those procedures will be used which facilitate the production of ideas and their clarification and understanding.

In a decision-making group, procedures will be used that clarify alternatives, bring the ethical implications of the Christian religion to bear in a relevant way, and aid the process of agreement. If the group has a redemptive function, the members will seek to relate themselves to others in ways that respect their integrity, recognize their worth as persons created in the image of God, and, through understanding, convey their own perception of the spiritual life of the other persons. If it is an action-taking group, the members will assume their fair share of responsibility for thinking out a Christian strategy and then assume their personal obligation to fulfill it.

## Roles of Members in a Discussion Group

As members perceive the need for specific functions, a group increases the quality of participation among members. In an effective discussion group, persons must ask vital, intelligent questions. These questions need to be formulated in such a way that there are real issues at stake. If the questions are loaded, persons usually know enough not to reply. If the questions are simply questions of fact, there can be little discussion. For example, there cannot be much discussion of the question, "Where was Paul born?" The question, "As he set out on his first missionary journey, do you think Paul was conscious of the fact that he was starting a new religion?" is a matter of one's opinion. One would have to gather evidence for his opinion from the reading of Paul's letters and the accounts in the book of Acts. It is an issue about which members of the class could have a discussion.

Asking intelligent questions is only one function that members must perform. There are many others. Persons in the group can bring interesting information. It needs to be relevant information. It can be based upon their experiences and their observations. It can be based upon their reading or their conversations with other persons. A group cannot get very far unless someone has data, evidence, facts, information, experiences, and other ideas to share.

As persons see the need, there is the occasion for summarizing what has been said so that persons do not repeat what has already been stated. At other points in the discussion, persons need to suggest a new strategy. Perhaps additional data is needed if the group is going to get somewhere with the subject. It may be that persons could view a film or a filmstrip and thus gain many new insights into their problem. The strategists might suggest this approach to the problem.

Occasionally persons get into a live argument in which there is a real division of opinion. Here the conciliators need to go to work so that persons may modify their opinions somewhat and come to a tentative agreement and the group may move on. Here are a minimum number of roles which members must assume if a group is going to be productive of ideas—question asker, information bringer, summarizer, conciliator, and strategist. Their participation in terms of these roles will depend upon their perception of what is needed. These skills can be learned as members of the group work at the process of thinking together.

## New Procedures in Groups

The ways that groups proceed depend upon the ends they seek. If they want members to master more of the ideas in the Bible, they may accomplish this by directed Bible reading and discussion in a better way than having someone talk to them about the Bible. If they want members of the group to make a decision, they must proceed in ways that will allow members to make decisions. When a group is failing to produce ideas or to suggest solutions to problems, its members need to re-evaluate the way they are proceeding. There is no magic formula for improving a group, but each group can change under its own self-direction. Here are some suggested procedures that tend to increase the participation of members.

### 1. DIRECTED BIBLE READING AND REPORTS

The leader will select certain passages which he wants the group to study. He will raise key questions concerning these passages and have them written on small slips of paper. As persons come to the classroom, he will give a slip of paper to two or three persons, asking them to look up this question and to interpret it to the group when he calls upon them. This can be done in five to seven minutes as a class begins its session.

Reading is a simple skill. We should encourage persons to do more of it in class. This calls for adequate lighting and the use of readable Bibles, books, and other resource materials. In this way all the members will be acquainted with the subject to be discussed. They will try out some of their ideas in the small group. They will filter out those that seem to be inconsequential and irrelevant. They will share their best insights with the larger group.

## 2. DRAMA AND DISCUSSION

The series of plays on family life produced by the Association for Mental Health, Inc., are excellent resources for a discussion of family-life problems. These plays may be read without rehearsal. As the reading of the play progresses, you may stop for discussion or wait until it is concluded and then evaluate the problems which the play presents. It is well to have resource persons sitting in the group and sharing their ideas. In this way many of the members will feel free to raise questions, and the resource person shares as he has an insight that is relevant to the problem under discussion.

## 3. FIELD TRIPS AND EVALUATION

This procedure involves going to a place, seeing what is going on, and thinking through its merits with the persons who have observed. Many religious groups support children's homes, old people's homes, and so on. A field trip to one of these homes where the members of the group seek to serve could be the basis for a good evaluation of the ways the church seeks to serve.

One day I was asked to lead a discussion with a group of interdenominational religious leaders on the values of camping. This was done easily because these leaders had been camping together for two weeks. They had observed it. They had experienced it. They could discuss it. It would have been foolish to talk about camping without having experienced it.

Here, for example, are some of the ideas shared in the discussion of spiritual values in camping.

Leader: Church camping is a community of Christians living out of doors. We judge our relationships with each other in the small camp group by the life and standards of Christ. Our group is a source of power in our lives. What spiritual values have you discovered in your experiences in your small camp group?

———: We found it a humbling experience. It revealed us as we really are, with all of our inadequacies, and yet each individual had an opportunity to contribute his share.

———: The gap between words and actions was narrowed in our small group as it can be narrowed in no other way. Artificial feelings were removed as each member got to know the others better.

———: There was the feeling on my own part that I must develop my own skills and abilities so that I might be able to make a better contribution to the group. I must make myself a better Christian so that I could give more.

———: The thing we feel is that in an outdoor setting we tend to be more creative than at other places. We usually think of the masses as a standard of success—to have lots of things going on, big things taking place. We think in terms of numbers. But, really, the most creative work that has been done in history has been done by small groups or by persons living in a setting of nature.

Leader: Let's move on into some of your activities in exploring nature round about us. Let's pursue that for a while and see some of the spiritual values we may have learned here.

———: Our group attempted to evaluate whether we received our more spiritual insights from the small group or from the out of doors. I think the combination of the small group and the out-of-doors living brings together values.

———: We discussed the fact that we have discovered

a oneness in all of life here. Living in the out of doors, we saw how God has provided for all of life, and we began to feel very much a part of the oneness of all creation.

————: Our group has talked about this at-homeness in God's world. Most persons, those coming from the cities particularly, would be afraid to go back into the woods and sleep alone for one night. When you begin to make out a *whole* to which you belong and over which God is the ruler, and you remember that he loves all of his creation, you are at home here.

————: Some may not agree, but I think the principle by which God works in one area is no different from the one by which he works in other areas. The highest example is the principle of the cross. The cross is not just a historic event but an eternal principle that works throughout creation. You can find example after example in your study of the out of doors.

————: Somehow this thought keeps running through my mind: In our job as Christian leaders, all this will have no value unless it is translated into everyday living and into the good life. While there may be those who will never be able to walk the paths or the roads to the top of the mountain, somehow we who have done so must be able to let them see an image of the good life.

————: Another point we learned was that there is beauty everywhere. We find more colors at our feet than we do when we look into the distance. Maybe we ought to teach people to find beauty in small things. We must never forget the beauty that is in people also.

Leader: I think we could go on and explore other areas where spiritual values have emerged. We might point out some of the vital spots where we could provide experiences that would change the lives of children, of youth, and of adults. I am amazed at the productivity of this group. Though we have gone a long way up the path this morning and have gained many significant insights, there are a lot of horizons out there ahead and we can keep pushing toward them.

## 4. LECTURE AND LISTENING GROUPS

If you have read the parable of the sower recently, you will recall that Jesus said, "His seeds fell on stony ground." Many a lecturer has felt that he had a good many rocks in his audience. Even the lecture process can be improved by the use of techniques that help to get members of the group involved in thinking as the person is speaking. Sometimes the audience is divided into listening groups. Some of the groups seek to discover ideas that need clarifying. Other groups discover ideas with which they disagree. Others find high points in the lecture which they would state as a summary.

As persons listen with a particular interest in mind, they tend to master more of the content. After the speaker has finished, they may ask him to clarify points that were confusing, they may state their disagreements and let him make his rebuttals, and they may summarize the main points which they have gathered from the speech. In this way, thinking will be stimulated more than in a one-way communication lecture process.

## 5. AUDIO-VISUALS AND AUDIENCE INVOLVEMENT

Before pictures are shown, it is interesting occasionally to ask persons to identify themselves with an individual in the movie. For example, if it is a biblical film, let them identify themselves with Paul or with other members in the council at Jerusalem. After the film, let persons discuss the main questions from the standpoint of the person they represent.

### 6. SOCIODRAMA AND HUDDLE GROUPS

Sociodrama is the spontaneous enactment by two or more persons of a social situation in which there is conflict of opinion or real differences in ways of behaving. Persons in the audience not only see the way they would act in a similar situation, but they begin to see what some of the results would be if they followed their inclinations.

In this manner persons may begin to change under their own self-direction, as they begin to foresee some of the consequences of the things they would do. For example, persons may enact the conflict between Jacob and Esau. This could get the members of the group into a discussion of this problem quite readily. Or a husband and wife could enact their different attitudes toward the way in which they should handle the question of discipline of their children. Through sociodrama we clarify alternate ways of behaving in these human situations and help persons in the group change as they envision some of the consequences of their actions.

After the sociodrama, persons can gather in huddle groups and discuss other alternatives and procedures and perhaps even test them if they have better solutions to the problem than the solution already portrayed.

### 7. NONVERBAL COMMUNICATION AND SMALL-GROUP DISCUSSION

This is the use of pantomime to portray certain feelings, such as loneliness. In training persons to visit I have asked persons to convey, without saying a word, how it feels to be a stranger alone in one's room, away from home, family, and friends. Through gestures, such as picking up the telephone, trying to write a letter, going to the window, pushing up the curtain, by expressing hope that someone will call and dejection when someone passes by, persons in the audience are made to feel very deeply what it is like to be alone. This procedure enables them to sharpen their perceptions greatly about the kind of approach they would make to a person in this situation when they call upon him to invite him to church.

In like manner I have asked parents to play with the toys in the nursery before we discuss the question, "What is it like to be a child in this church school?"

Through the use of religious symbols we can convey much meaning. Many a lesson can be approached nonverbally if the proper symbols are put into focus in the classroom.

## 8. ROLE PLAYING AND BUZZ GROUPS

Role playing is a spontaneous enactment of a way of behaving on the part of one or more persons. For example, a young housewife with small children may act out the way she feels at the end of a day in which she has tried to provide adequately for her family.

A buzz group is a small group of two or three persons. They do not have a leader. They will simply talk over a question, such as "How do you handle fatigue when it seems to be getting the best of you?" The discussion of this question would naturally follow the role-playing incident of the housewife. After members of the group have talked it over informally, they would share their best insights with the rest of the group.

## 9. SYMPOSIUM OR PANEL DISCUSSION

A symposium is used when a person wants to present two or three points of view to the group for discussion. It is very helpful in clarifying alternatives. The members of the symposium make short speeches. When they have had a chance to state their points of view clearly, members of the audience begin to question them for purposes of clarification. After this, the whole group may engage in a discussion of the central issues, and two or three persons may be appointed to summarize.

A symposium differs from a panel discussion at this point. A panel is led by a moderator who asks leading questions. Members of the panel all comment on these questions. They may ask further questions of one another for purposes of clarification but there are no set speeches. Many a so-called panel discussion has really been a symposium. After members of the panel have commented on questions the moderator usually summarizes and moves on to the next point. Members of the audience may ask questions of the moderator. He refers them to members of the panel. In the end the moderator summarizes the main points discussed.

## 10. REALITY TESTING

Occasionally there is need to test our ideas. When members of the group merely give a generalized solution to a problem, we need to apply it specifically to a case. This may be done by having persons role play the solution to their problems and letting others evaluate it or try different solutions.

For example, groups may conclude that when cocktails are passed at a party, they should say "no." This is a good intention, but the next step is learning to say "no" under varying circumstances. How do you do it when you have been invited to the boss's house? A group could role play this incident, showing how they can keep their convictions, maintain wholesome personal relations with the boss, and not sacrifice their own integrity.

## 11. EVALUATION

Members of a group need to stop occasionally and evaluate how well they are attaining the ends which they seek. Sometimes such a simple process as asking persons what are the weaknesses and what are the strong points of this meeting will lead to suggestions for improvement.

### Tasks of a Group Observer

Some groups are introducing a new type of leader to help them see more clearly the way the group is operating. He is known as the group observer. His job is to help the group become aware of its procedures. He considers himself a member of the group, but he watches skillfully what the group is doing. He may chart the course of the conversation, record the roles that members have fulfilled, and diagram patterns of participation. The process of reporting to the group is known as the "feed back."

The group observer does not take notes on the contents of the discussion. Rather, he watches the procedures. He observes the way the group gets started, the way the members participate, and the way they help one another in discovering solutions to problems. An observer works out an analysis concerning the way the group behaves and reports it to the group. He may note the ability of the group to produce ideas, make decisions, handle conflicts, and produce solutions.

The observer works with the group. He participates in it, yet tries to be objective about the way the group operates. He reports his observations in a wholesome manner. He should not attract attention to himself nor try to be defensive. He must be clear or he will create confusion. He must never use the role of observer to show how superior his methods are to those of the group. He may give such comments as, "In discussing this question we spent so much time on such and such a plan." Or he may produce a drawing and say, "At this point our pattern of participation was like this . . ." With this kind of report the group can begin to correct itself. The observer is not the corrector.

Here is the report of an observer after watching a group get started in a discussion. This group had assigned one person to lead their thinking on a particular issue. The brackets around the number indicate the observer's estimate of the way the leader started.

## A GROUP OBSERVER'S REPORT
*Initiating the Discussion*

| 3 | [2] | 1 | 0 | 1 | 2 | 3 |
|---|-----|---|---|---|---|---|
| Group needed more help | | | Right amount of help | | | Group needed less help |

Climate-Making: Encourage Christian fellowship
Permissive
Encourage participation

| 3 | 2 | [1] | 0 | 1 | 2 | 3 |
|---|---|---|---|---|---|---|
| Group needed help to secure permissive atmosphere | | | Right amount of help | | | Group needed less help |

As the discussion between members and the leader began, the observer noted the roles that members assumed when they began to participate.

### Roles Played by Persons in the Group

| Roles | Persons | Number of Times Assumed Role |
|---|---|---|
| Asked Questions: | A | 1 |
| | B | 1 |
| | C | 1 |
| | D | 1 |
| | E | 1 |
| | G | 2 |
| Clarifier: | F | 1 |
| | G | 2 |
| Brought Information: | B | 3 |
| | D | 1 |
| | E | 1 |
| | G | 1 |
| | H | 1 |
| | I | 1 |
| | J | 2 |
| Summarizer: | F | 1 |

At two different intervals the observer recorded the patterns of participation. By evaluating them the members of the group discovered ways to improve their contribution to the group.

The first observation appeared thus:

*Participation Chart I*

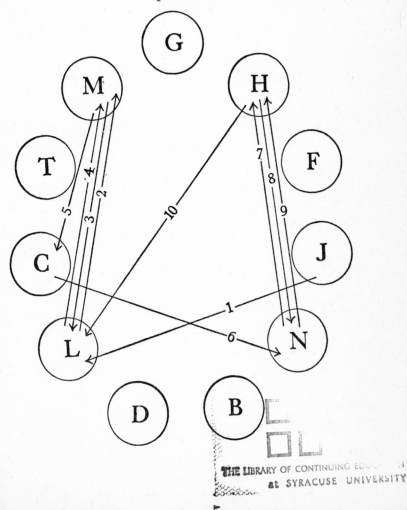

At another juncture, two persons became involved in a clash and the conversation pattern for about five minutes went like this:

*Participation Chart II*

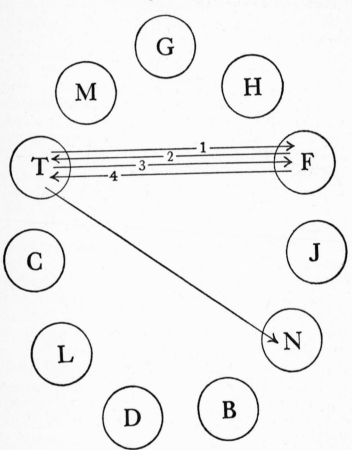

Obviously, any group viewing these participation charts could discern quickly the difficulties faced and seek to correct them. The observer merely reports what goes on in the process of thinking. The group evaluates this information periodically. It may be of value to present the observer's report at the beginning of a new session so that members of the group may use it to improve their ways of participating in the next discussion.

## Groups Change Through Self-Evaluation

Through self-evaluation the members of a group can change. They can awaken each other to the Christian goals they seek, increase productivity of ideas, and clarify alternatives before them in making basic decisions. They create the conditions wherein people may change under their own volition. They can begin those practices that will bring about a more dynamic relationship between their members and Christ.

Every adult group in the church school can evaluate itself with greater accuracy today. Through personal discipline individuals may allow the spiritual factors in the Christian religion to have greater influence in their own lives and in the lives of others. As persons master the "language of relationships," they can help others to change under their own self-discipline. In this manner "the word" becomes the living word—vital, alive, energizing the lives of members of the group. Each man of faith is a priest to the other members, mediating the spirit of Christ to them.

The Christian grows in the life of faith as he discusses its implications for his job, his family relationships, his place of service in the church, and his responsibilities in the world. All of these experiences need to be related to God as he has been revealed in Christ. The effectiveness of these discussions can be improved by the use of new methods of evaluation used in groups.

## PROJECTS FOR STUDY AND ACTION

1. Outline a lecture on "The Dead Sea Scrolls," "The First Missionary Journey of Paul," or some other topic of your choosing. The purpose is to impart information. The following Sunday present the group with a ten-point true or false test. How much did the listeners retain for one week? Next week try another lecture. This time divide the class into listening groups. Test again. Compare results.

2. Introduce a new study unit by having members of the group read biblical passages and discover answers to questions on the passages. Have them report and interpret their answers. The next week, test the group (true or false) for a mastery of these ideas. Compare the amount of correct answers with the experiment suggested in No. 1.

3. Role play three different attitudes toward a current international situation. Ask the group to suggest solutions for it.

4. Assign members various roles, such as question-asker, bringer of information, summarizer, reconciler, strategist, clarifier, and group observer. Discuss the topic: "Which way to church unity is best?" Ask the group observer to report.

5. Choose a lesson from your curriculum materials. State your aims in discussing it. Outline the procedures you would use to increase group participation. Why? How would they help the group achieve the aim of the lesson?

# BIBLIOGRAPHY

1. Adler, Mortimer J. *How to Read a Book*. New York: Simon & Schuster, Inc., 1940. A discussion of the psychology of reading.

2. Auer, J. Jeffrey, and Ewbank, Henry Lee. *Handbook for Discussion Leaders*. New York: Harper & Bros., 1954. A descriptive analysis of the basic techniques in leading a discussion.

3. Bales, R. F. *Interaction Process Analysis*. Cambridge, Mass.: Addison-Wesley Publishing Co., 1950. A method for the study of small groups.

4. Cantor, Nathaniel. *The Teaching-Learning Process*. New York: Dryden Press, 1953. A discussion of the reality-centered school, functions of the teacher, personal involvements in learning, and basic tenets of learning.

5. Haiman, F. S. *Group Leadership and Democratic Action*. Boston: Houghton Mifflin Co., 1951. Discusses basic attitudes and skills of democratic leadership of discussion groups.

6. "How to Conduct a Discussion." 16 mm. film with sound, 25 minutes, b. & w. *Encyclopaedia Britannica*. Illustrates eleven basic principles for the guidance of discussions.

7. Kelley, Earl C. *The Workshop Way of Learning*. New York: Harper & Bros., 1951. A description of basic principles and procedures of this way of learning, which places basic responsibility on the student.

8. Kuhn, M. E. *You Can't Be Human Alone*. New York: National Council of Churches, 1956. A descriptive and illustrative statement of good group procedures.

9. Lee, Irving J. *How to Talk with People*. New York: Harper & Bros., 1952. An excellent treatment of our ways of averting misunderstandings and conflicts and improving our understandings of people.

10. Strauss, Bert and Frances. *New Ways to Better Meetings*. New York: Viking Press, 1951. Excellent suggestions for improving group meetings. Good material for leaders.

CHAPTER VI

# Communicating the Gospel

THIS IS THE AGE OF COMMUNICATION. WE POSSESS MORE powerful gadgets to transmit ideas than any nation in history. Radio, television, the press, pour out daily an undigestible quantity of ideas, notions, and opinions. Yet we seem to understand each other less. Why? Is communication more than the powerful transmission of ideas?

*Communication Is a Two-Way Street*

While listening to an address one day, I heard the person next to me mutter, "Brother, you are not communicating with me." With that statement he turned off the listening part of his mind and started to think about something else. Why does this practice prevail so largely today?

Perhaps two illustrations will help us understand the reasons for the breakdown in communication between persons.

On one occasion I listened to a group of farmers discussing what they should do about the drop in wheat prices. They talked about the surpluses and ways of distributing them. They talked about the value of limiting acreage and the failures in administering such a plan. Whether they were growing wheat or had the larger proportion of their acreage in other crops, they all joined in the discussion. It was a common problem. They were all involved in its solution. They were communicating with one another about it.

A few days later I visited a large city and had luncheon with another group of men. This time the conversation was vastly different. No matter what subject was discussed, the majority of those present were not interested. They formed little conversation groups on the side. Each was a specialist in his own field. He could not get out of it. He was unable to communicate when they were not talking his language, about his problems, his particular area of specialization.

Although the cities have brought about 90 per cent of the Americans together geographically, they have increased the difficulties of communication. Think of the persons on your street. When they go to work on Monday morning, each person goes to a different job, does a different though specialized type of work. Each person must know more and more about his work. This drive toward specialization has increased the chasm of differences between us so that when we try to communicate, we sometimes feel like a person trying to shout across the Grand Canyon; our own words keep coming back to us.

In real communication there is a genuine relationship set up between at least two people. It is a two-way street. There is a meeting of mind and spirit. Each individual is not transmitting his ideas from his own isolated booth. There is a positive attempt to share experiences, clarify meanings, and develop understandings between two or more persons. Without this effort on the part of persons, there may be a noisy monologue but little or no communication.

In real communication there is also a clear understanding of, and agreement concerning, the goals to be reached and the procedures to be used in reaching them. Even in conventions, where large numbers of people make up the audience, they need to be helped in knowing what to listen for and how to participate in the meeting. In this kind of meeting leaders may be designated to help the audience focus its listening and guide its participation. In an adult group the president may perform this function or it may be done by the director of study and worship.

Communication takes place in an adult group when persons can identify the love of God with their own personal need. In the Incarnation, God became flesh in a very real way. He moved into our community. He began to live among us. He revealed that his true character was love. It was the kind of love that no anxiety could destroy, even when that anxiety drove all of Christ's followers into seclusion and prompted his enemies to destroy him.

Today the church is the body of Christ. We are the incarnation of the Holy Spirit. He is our eternal guide. Either we communicate this spirit to others in our groups or their lives will be impoverished. Remember not all communication is verbal. When the Quakers meet and listen for the inner promptings of the Holy Spirit, they are communicating. When they are guided by the inner light, they become the most illuminated souls on this world's darkened horizon.

*Barriers to Communication*

1. *Irrelevancy.* Communication in a Christian study group breaks down when members assume that the Christian message is unrelated to their lives. Here is one of the most difficult tasks of the leader. He must remain true to the gospel message. This message took shape in a Greco-Roman world over nineteen centuries ago, yet it must be related to the spiritual needs of twentieth-century persons. How? This dilemma can

never be overcome by a group leader alone. Members must participate as the "priesthood of believers," as Protestantism has always alleged. They must be quick to discern the relevant truths. They must seek to relate them to the spiritual condition of members of the group.

2. *Anxiety*. Sometimes the channels of communication get jammed through heightened anxieties on the part of one or more persons in a group. Anxiety is a nameless fear. It strikes at the very core of one's being. Its object is to destroy the soul. When persons are seized by it, they withdraw. They resist others. They may begin to suspect or devaluate others. They fail to listen to others and are very quick to defend their own ideas. They may become hostile toward others and even set off a conflict with them. These feelings of fear and fight break down communication.

3. *Mobility*. The high rate of mobility among adults, especially among young adults, makes communication in an adult group difficult. It tends to increase a feeling of rejection. They feel that they don't belong anywhere; they are rootless. Joseph Sittler has described their situation with incisive accuracy.

A young man is born in Ohio, goes to school in Massachusetts, marries a girl from Virginia. Their first child is born in the Bronx, baptized in a church that knew them not as children and will not see them in old age. The young father goes to work in Manhattan for a corporation chartered in Delaware, writes advertisements for the consumption of people he never sees and for whom he has no immediate responsibility. And at any time he may and probably will be ordered to move in two weeks to Dallas, Texas, there to pick up certain contacts (how expressive a word that, for the way we moderns meet one another!) that will be useful to him when after two years he is transferred to Seattle, Washington.[1]

This process depersonalizes life. It dulls our judgments about the values of persons. These persons react to others as if they were stereotypes. One never really gets to know and appreciate the value of other persons. He never feels that they are interested in what he believes.

The Gospels are filled with relevant words for this person. Wayne E. Oates asserts:

In His parables, Jesus repeatedly dealt with the problem of alienation, excommunication, and dissociation within the community of the house of Israel. He told of the wheat and the tares growing together; he told of the ninety-nine sheep safely in the fold, and the one separated from them. He told of the ostracized and ostracizing sons; he told of the Good Samaritan. The broken cord of communication was the common theme of all these stories. He gave himself redemptively to the bridging of that gap.[2]

4. *Confusion.* A further barrier needs to be surmounted if effective communication is going to take place in an adult group. We must overcome the confusion centering on those religious symbols that express the meanings of our religious experiences. Some persons identify their religious experiences so closely with a particular time, place, and culture that these symbols become meaningless when the situations and the culture changes. Persons who identify their experience of God with an aristocratic, medieval, legalistic, punitive, completely

[1] "Meant for Each Other," *Motive*, December, 1955, p. 6. Used by permission.

[2] "Counseling and Communication," *Religious Education*, March-April, 1955, p. 105. Used by permission of the publisher.

stratified and frozen society have a hard time trying to understand a God of love who seeks to redeem life. Their difficulty lies in the set of symbols they use to think about God. There is a very delicate balance between the justice, love, and redemptive power of God, and any real understanding of him is based on an adequate understanding of the symbols that represent these aspects of his being.

The focal symbol of the Christian religion is the cross. This symbol does not merely refer to an event in human history. It refers to the redeeming love and saving power of God. This is the great truth that ultimately matters in human history. Although it occurred at one time and place in history, its meaning is eternal and relevant at all times and in all places. God made the greatest sacrifice anyone could make to reconcile us to him. We never need to walk alone. We are "at one" with him.

This is the meaning of the Atonement. It can open the door to vital experiences with God which will transform us. We too can overcome the sins of attitude, prejudice, and hatred just as Christ did—by absorbing them and getting rid of them. We too can *atone* for evil. This is one meaning of the symbol of the cross.

## Our Common Union with God

In real communication of the Christian gospel, these barriers of anxiety, mobility, irrelevancy, and confusion need to be overcome. Through the gospel a person discovers what God has done for man in Christ. He responds by renewing his own personal relationships to the God whom Christ revealed and to his fellow men. Edward T. Ramsdell states:

There can be no real communication of the Gospel apart from our real concern for others, and any real concern for others is self communication. It is a reaching out to them, not merely at the intellectual level, but at the level of depth of our common being, where we feel our need of God and where the grace of God becomes an experienced reality. . . . It is at such a level, and only here, that we ever come truly to realize our unity in Christ.[3]

Through the renewal that begins in prayer one can re-establish a right relationship to God, because God's seeking love wants to reconcile us to him. In the Christian religion our common union with God is the basis of the gospel we communicate.

We can help to overcome anxiety and confusion by our ability to listen to and understand others. We have little to communicate until we can do so. Other persons must relate new ideas and experiences to the ones they already have if these new ideas are going to have meaning for their lives. As persons listen to others, they can relate their ideas in meaningful ways and can convey a relevant word of understanding.

Communication is more than using the correct word symbols. It means bringing life into the classroom so that persons may experience the redeeming love of God at work in human relationships.

How would you go about trying to provide an experience wherein adults could clarify the meanings of the religious experiences that they associate with the cross? Here are some suggestions of the author to students of the International Lesson Series. Would these suggestions enable a group to communicate the gospel to its members during a class session?

[3] "Communication from a Christian Perspective," *Religious Education*, September-October, 1955, p. 339.

# Unit VIII: The Lord of Life

*Lesson 4: The Meaning of Christ's Suffering*[4]

Luke 23:20-46

The heart of the gospel is the message of salvation through the death and Resurrection of Christ. This revealing act prompts our faith in the love of God. It is the saving act that saves us from the crushing blows of fear that would destroy our souls. It is the source of our hope. It is the source of the spiritual power of the Christian life.

Completely overcome by jealousy, hatred, secret scheming, injustice, mob violence, and the collective plots of men of power, Jesus reveals that the love of God is invincible. God deals with men according to the ways of his own nature, not by their whims. He deals with them according to the ways of creative power, moral goodness, and redemptive love. Ultimately, he determines the destiny of men.

This morning, suppose the leader guides the whole group in a discussion of this lesson. Distribute Bibles and the lesson materials to the members. Develop the lesson around these three central questions:

1. What sins do we see revealed in the Crucifixion story?

Have persons read some of the biblical passages. Let others pinpoint the sins by which we are victimized, such as:

"He stirs up the people." Do we avoid controversy at all cost when we hear someone make this statement?

"Release to us Barabbas." How many times each week do we yield to the pressure of the crowd in this highly propagandized society?

"What shall I do with Jesus?" Do we sin through indecision?

2. How does Jesus deliver us from sin?

Physically overwhelmed, Jesus upon the cross uttered, "Father, forgive them; for they know not what they do." This statement was a continuation of his previous acts of forgiveness. These acts had been contested by the religious hierarchy of Israel, yet Jesus remained true to this attitude. He knew that men would need a new spiritual center for life so that they could make a new start in their spiritual development. In this way he saved us from the implacable web of evil into a new beginning in life.

Let the group discuss this question: "How does Jesus' death upon the cross save us from sin within our souls and from the forces of evil that oppress us?"

3. What are the conditions of our forgiveness if we are to begin life anew with Christ? What is repentance? What kind of attitudes and relationships does one establish toward one's fellow men? What willful acts are necessary upon our part to demonstrate that the grace of God is at work within us as it was within Christ?

This lesson can end with a worship experience in which the members thank God for the gift of his Son, for the saving power that he brings, and may renew their trust in him for their own deliverance from anxiety, fear, and death.


Communication involves the ability to enter with understanding into the experiences of other people, to feel as they feel, to see life as they see it. When we do so, we give up something of ourselves but we gain deeper wisdom.

One evening, at a conference on Christian education, the speaker was giving an address on the clause from the Lord's Prayer "Thy will be done." Prior to his speaking, four persons had presented a brief sociodrama. It focused the attention of the entire audience of more than 750 persons on the problem of a director of religious education who was deciding whether to remain in his present job or to accept an invitation to a larger church. After being appealed to by his group to take care of "number one" first, by his conscience to renew his commitment to the call of service, by his wife to think of giving the children the opportunities they needed, he replied with the question, "How do you decide what is the will of God for you?"

Following the leadership of Paul Maves, the conference divided into small groups of six persons to discuss this question for about eight minutes. In the small group in which I participated, the following insights were stated:

"I think of the great Christians of our age: Schweitzer, Kagawa, McConnell, Jones. Then I ask, 'I wonder how they would handle this problem.'"

"I may take two or three weeks to work out a solution. I'll read the Bible, trying to find relevant passages, and I'll talk with friends that I trust."

"Prayer. I spend some time praying about it."

"Inevitably there comes a time when I must launch out with faith and try the new insight."

"Many times I have started something new. When I received help in many ways from God, I knew it was his will. When I did not feel renewed, strengthened, and guided, I knew it was mine."

At this point time ran out. We reassembled with the convention audience. Yet our minds were stirred; we were seeking to know the will of God.

In this setting the speaker began his address on "Thy will be done." When he finished, the young man next to me said, "He was really communicating with me. I think there are a few decisions I had better make tonight."

## Communicating the Gospel Implies

Although there are many others, at least these conditions are essential in the communication process:

Communicating the Christian gospel is a task that calls for an understanding of the inner dynamics of listening and participation, overcoming the barriers of resistance and confusion, and mastering the skills in interpersonal relations.

Communication depends upon a genuine two-way relationship being established between people so that they may share experiences and understand meanings as persons.

Communication of the gospel begins to take place when persons in the group identify the goals of their lives with the goals of the gospel.

Communication in the Christian community places responsibility on the part of the one sharing the insight to relate it to the spiritual condition of the members of the group, recognizing his own need of the grace of God and the sufficiency of God's grace for all persons.

Communication implies involvement of persons in the redemptive process. There can be no real communication of the gospel unless we have a genuine and sacrificial concern for others.

Communication implies a process of clarification and the understanding of meanings that are related to the religious experiences of persons. Each adult will relate the new meaning to his former experiences. Leaders need to provide situations where they may have new religious experiences so that the gospel will acquire new meaning and power in their lives.

# PROJECTS FOR STUDY AND ACTION

1. Formulate your own theory of communication based on your reading, experience, and reflection.

2. Jim Hansen is a real go-getter. He likes to champion a cause. He uses these situations, however, to project his hostility onto others. How would you convey to Jim your understanding of him and at the same time help him become a better Christian?

3. Bill and Gloria Mead have moved, moved, moved. They resist coming to the adult group in your church. They have been hurt in past associations. You are assigned to visit them. How would you communicate a real feeling of acceptance to them?

4. Last Sunday a person with epilepsy visited with your group. As she sat down, the persons around her shrank away from her. How would you proceed to talk over this problem in a class meeting to help the fearful persons? What would you do to communicate the real Christian spirit which your group would like to extend toward this person?

5. How would you proceed in class to help persons discover for themselves the meaning of Christ's death?

6. How would you help members of the group discover God's will for their lives?

## BIBLIOGRAPHY

1. Benne, K. D. "How Does Communication Take Place?" *Religious Education*, L (September-October, 1955), 331-34. A brief article defining the tasks in communication.
2. Cauter, T., and Downham, J. S. *The Communication of Ideas*. London: Chatto & Windus, 1954. A study of influences upon and barriers to communication in present-day urban life.

3. Chase, Stuart. *The Power of Words*. New York: Harcourt, Brace, & Co., 1954. A study of language and the use of words in swaying public opinion.

4. Festinger, L., and Thibaut, J. W. "Interpersonal Communication in Small Groups," *Journal of Abnormal and Social Psychology*, XLVI (1951), 92-99. An article describing experiments in conformity and deviation in small groups.

5. Flesch, Rudolph. *The Art of Plain Talk*. New York: Harper & Bros., 1946. How to use the English language. Composition.

6. Howland, C. J., *et al. Communication and Persuasion*. New Haven, Conn.: Yale University Press, 1954. A study of opinion change through persuasion.

7. Hyde, R. W. "Communication of Feeling in Group Psychotherapy," *Journal of Pastoral Care*, VI (Fall, 1952), 26-33. A study of empathy in establishing good person-to-person relationships.

8. Katz, Elihu, and Lazarsfield, Paul. *Personal Influence*. Glencoe, Ill.: Free Press, 1955. The effects of individual personality in mass communications.

9. Oates, Wayne E., *et al.* "Communicating the Gospel," *Religious Education*, L (March-April, 1955), 103-21. A symposium on communication through counseling and interpersonal relationships.

10. Ramsdell, E. T. "Communication from a Christian Perspective," *Religious Education*, L (September-October, 1955), 335-39. A theological view of what takes place in communication.

# CHAPTER VII

# Learning Is Person to Person

REAL LEARNING INVOLVES CHANGE. IT IS CHANGE IN KNOWL-edge, concepts, and understandings. It means that an individual may change what he knows about the Bible and how he conceives of Christ, and that he may alter his own understanding of the purpose of the church. It involves changing attitudes so that a person's love toward God and his fellow men may become enlarged and more inclusive. It involves helping people to manage their human relationships so that they will treat others as if they are spiritual beings. In this exciting process of adult learning, spiritual values become the central determining factors in one's life. This inner field of spiritual power influences our choices and guides our actions.

This insight is crucial in learning the Christian way of life. If that way of life is going to be shared, then persons need to relate themselves to others as persons in such a way that they may understand the other person and respond to him as a person. In our society we are experts at relating ourselves to other people as if they are things. Our greatest problems emerge when we try to relate ourselves to others as persons. We fail, as Martin Buber puts it, when we leave the world of "it" and enter into the world of "thou." In this world persons are not statistics to be weighed, measured, judged, and controlled. Rather, a person is a self, a soul, an independent center of intelligence, moral will, and spiritual power.

## God Is Personally Related to Us

It seems to me that this is the kind of relationship which God established with the world when he sent his son Jesus Christ into it. He chose to enter into our experiences as human beings. He moved into a house on our street. This is the meaning of the Incarnation which forms the foundation for the Christian approach to our knowledge of God. As Christ dwelt among men, he established the intellectual and spiritual bonds between himself and his followers that enabled him to reveal what God was like. These new insights became the basis of the Christian faith, commitment, and source of power in the lives of men. Thus the foundation of Christian learning is person to person.

Likewise persons may learn the Christian way of life through the quality of the relationships between persons in adult groups in the church school today. Within the groups they have abundant opportunities to discover that they are spiritual beings who have an inner guide of faith and power for their lives. This discernment is a gift, the gift of the Holy Spirit. It is clearly discerned when persons apprehend that an individual's life is inwardly controlled by love, joy, peace, understanding, kindness, and patience. Francis J. McConnell once put it this way: "Some lives themselves *mean* truths which we discern as soon as we come into touch with the lives. Some faces mean and teach purity the instant we look upon them. Words would be superfluous and impertinent." [1]

[1] *Personal Christianity* (New York: Fleming H. Revell Co., 1914), p. 19.

Within adult groups in the church school, persons reveal the Christian quality of their own lives or the lack of it. They may reveal that they are basically insecure people who continuously project their anxieties onto other people. In fact, the vehemence with which they project them may reveal the depth of the insecurity in their own natures. They may reveal that they are persons in whom the spirit of Christ dwells, or they may reveal that they are so possessed of inner hatreds that they must go about expressing prejudgments, making violent remarks, or committing acts of temper. They may become gracious persons through whom God's redeeming love flows as a field of magnetic power or they may be self-centered creatures who are caught in a web of their own egocentricity.

## Learning the Christian Way

There is much more to learning the Christian way of life than discovering the attitudes of Christian persons—that is, those attitudes which speak more loudly than our theological concepts. Christian learning on a mature level takes place as persons learn to establish their own Christ-controlled relations to other people.

The clarity of Martin Buber's insight at this point is illuminating: "The true community does not arise through people's having feelings for one another (though indeed not without it), but through, first, their taking their stand in living mutual relation with a living centre, and, second, their being in living mutual relation with one another." [2]

Here is the core of the matter. It is within the Christian

[2] *I and Thou* (New York: Chas. Scribner's Sons, 1937), p. 45.

fellowship, where the two or three are gathered together in the name of Christ, that his spirit becomes a dynamic, guiding factor in the life of a person. It is here that a person meets the Christ of his own experience and works out his own faith and way of life, according to his own understanding of the meaning of Christ's life for himself.

This is not a passive way of learning. It is an encounter that goes on deep within the soul of a man. It is person-to-person communication.

Emil Brunner says:

And likewise in faith I do not think, but God leads me to think; He does not communicate "something" to me, but "Himself." The counterpart is no longer as in thinking a something, a something pondered and discussed which I infer through the energy of my thinking, but a Person who Himself speaks and discloses Himself, who Himself thus has the initiative and guidance and takes over the role . . . which in thinking I have myself. An exchange hence takes place here which is wholly without analogy in the sphere of thinking. The sole analogy is in the encounter between human beings, the meeting of person with person.[3]

In this kind of learning through personal encounter, God who was in Christ establishes a reconciling relationship with you. He enables the person to change from ego-centeredness to Christ-centeredness and to work out new attitudes and relationships in life from this new point of reference. The spirit of Christ bears witness with our own spirit. It reassures us that we are the sons of God.

[3] *The Divine-Human Encounter* (Philadelphia: Westminster Press, 1943), p. 85. Used by permission of the author.

## Our Personal Relation to Christ

Individuals who come to know the God of our Lord and Savior Jesus Christ in a personal way will encounter him many times in their lives. This is an encounter with redeeming love. Jesus Christ did not merely reveal the concept of redeeming love as an idea, but he made it flesh incarnate. He communicated this redeeming love in a personal way. It is part of our blood corpuscles and body cells. It is in society as a cohesive and faith-engendering force. It seeks to save us from pride to humble service. It seeks to save us from a life of anxiety and protest to a life of faith and trust. It seeks to save us from man-made catastrophe to God-made peace. It is encountered whenever we seek to live the Christ-centered life of faith.

## A Love-controlled Life

The life of maturing Christian love is learned as a person seeks to control his own relationships with other persons, as if other persons were children of God and as if he were a channel through which the love of God could reach them. Findings of psychology and psychiatry make it apparent that a person must have a wholesome attitude toward himself before he can love others in a wholesome way. The person who hates himself will seek to impose his hatred upon others.

"The courage to be in this respect is the courage to accept the forgiveness of sins, not as an abstract assertion but as a fundamental experience in the encounter with God," states Paul Tillich. "No self acceptance is possible if one is not accepted in a person-to-person relation." [4] Thus the person who

[4] *The Courage to Be* (London: James Nisbet & Co., 1953), pp. 156-57.

has a person-to-person experience of Christian learning regains a sense of his own worth as a child of God. He will not want to exploit or impose his ideas, his way of life, or his plan of action on others.

This truth is just as applicable in the area of social relations between nations. It is the victimized, the undernourished, the poorly clad, the disease-ridden peoples that seek to vindicate their plight through aggression.

The knowledge that a God of love seeks to establish right relationships with us is the most imperative truth for our time. It alone can restore to us a right image of our true selves. It alone can renew a right spirit within us.

This knowledge cannot be learned simply by hearing someone speak to us. It is personal knowledge and comes only through persons who communicate that love to the inner personal region of other persons. It is learned in our living relationships. It is learned in those acts that enable one person to relate himself to another as a brother. In this manner the "tie that binds our hearts in Christian love" becomes the cohesive cords that hold society together. If God sent forth his son "in the fullness of time" to reveal his true nature to mankind, the whole of creation is surely awaiting the advent of the sons of God today. These sons must reveal that the love of God is stronger than temporal coalitions of military power that threaten to destroy our planet.

We climb the ladder of love one rung at a time—wholesome self-love, brotherly love, self-sacrificing and humbly serving love. Curious, isn't it? We are born into the world completely dependent creatures. We want everything. We must be waited on continuously or we cannot survive. We are tummy-centered. We make our wishes known in very audible ways.

No wonder it is so difficult to get us to outgrow our self-centeredness and to become aware that others around us are persons, not objects for our use or manipulation. If, then, we find it difficult to treat our neighbor as a brother, how much more difficult it is to sacrifice to help starving, disease-ridden peoples in other lands whom we have never seen. Yet this is the direction of our growth in Christian love if we are to fulfill the destiny appointed for us.

## A Laboratory in Human Relationships

If adults are going to learn to communicate a quality of mature Christian love, classes and groups need to become laboratories in human relationships. Members need to be guided in practicing the art of accepting the grace of God and of relating themselves to their fellow men in ways that aid God in the process of redemption. This means relating ourselves to others as persons so that they come to an awareness of their own reality as persons, the sons and daughters of God.

The Gospels are replete with citations of the ways that Jesus related himself to others so as to bring them to a right relationship to God. Zacchaeus was a man with plenty of economic security obtained at the cost of the hatred and distrust of his fellow men. Through his relationship to Christ he established a new relationship to God and then set about working out a new set of right relationships with his fellow men. After the healing of the Gerasene demoniac Jesus saw that the man was becoming completely and absolutely dependent on him. When the man asked Jesus whether he could join the disciples and stay by his side, Jesus commanded this person who had been restored to a new wholesome faith to return to his own village, where people had jeered at him. By so doing he could become a free spiritual being who was starting to walk the hard road toward spiritual maturity. Only in this manner could he develop the potential powers that were in him. In both of these instances Jesus was relating himself to these men in a redemptive way. Zacchaeus became worth something for God when he gave up his idolatry of things. Likewise the Gerasene demoniac became worth something for God when he went back to the town where men feared him and lived a life of trust in God.

So it is in adult classes! When we relate ourselves to others in such a way that the love of God can reach them through us, they change. Perhaps the hardest task we have as religious person is to accept ourselves. We want to accept some idealized image of what we are. This tends to make us distort the impression we have of other persons because we don't resemble the idealized image of ourselves. We surely don't dare consider that they are better than we are. Until we realize that God accepts us as we are, we cannot change. When we do realize it, we can talk to him in prayer, renew our true relationship to him, and begin to receive his gracious pardon.

Forgiveness is a mutual relationship between ourselves and God and between ourselves and our fellow men. It is hard to forgive others if we do not accept the fact that God has forgiven us. When we accept the fact that he has, our thoughts, attitudes, and actions begin to change. It is easier to accept others. The ability to accept others enables persons in a Christian fellowship to establish a reconciling relationship to one's fellow men. This is our ultimate task in Christian adult education. It is not enough to communicate the ideas of the gospel. That is good in itself, but it is not enough. We must mediate the love and acceptance of God through the way we relate ourselves to others. Real maturity is based on this kind of giving of love even when one does not get it in return, simply because this is the way we relate ourselves to God. "Forgiveness," says Carroll A. Wise, "given and received, is an essential experience in becoming our real selves, as that in us which leads us not to forgive nor to accept forgiveness is not our real self, but a well defended weakness in ourselves." [5]

## The Adult Group: A Redemptive Fellowship

The members of an adult group who look upon their educational task as redemptive will seek to help persons accept others because they are of real worth to God. They will seek to relate these persons to Christ in such a way that he will become a dynamic power in their lives. They will not talk simply about what they read he has done in the past; they will seek to be guided by his spirit and to indicate to others that they have a living relation to him. They will seek to create the climate in the group wherein persons can change to bring their attitudes, actions, and habits in compliance with the spirit of Christ. Members of the group will seek to reinforce the persons in their changes so that "fruits of the spirit" may abide in their souls. As persons gain self-discipline through a love-controlled life, they will perceive more quickly the spiritual needs of others and will respond with vitality and insight with which God the Creator and Redeemer ever renews our souls.

[5] *Psychiatry and the Bible* (New York: Harper & Bros., 1956), p. 109.

## Worship and Learning

As the dynamic process of person-to-person learning advances, there will be many occasions when members feel that they want to express in a total way their experience of the worth of God in their lives. Out of the experience of trust toward one another that develops, persons may come to place their ultimate trust in God. Through many insights into new experiences they become aware of God in their lives.

This recognition calls for a total response of their whole being to God in worship. Through the renewal of spiritual power that comes from a sense of being reconciled to God, a person may want to express his own inner gratitude to God. As individuals make decisions, they may seek a new spiritual power to guide and strengthen them in carrying out the choices which they have made. Thus the experience of worship grows out of this heightened learning on a new level. Members want to join with the whole congregation to express the worth of God in their lives. Through this process the group seeks to create the conditions wherein worship becomes a meaningful experience.

It is the opinion of Wesner Fallaw that

Religious education that eventuates in worship has to interrelate its forms of training with experiences in which reconciliation, justice and love develop new persons in Christ. . . . Learning to worship, giving evidence that education in Christianity has actually caused men to grow sufficiently in order to have that mind which was also in Christ Jesus, is the immediate need and final objective of religious education that is centered in Christ.[6]

[6] "The Function of Groups in Learning Christianity," *Religious Education,* November-December, 1950, p. 330.

Learning that involves person-to-person relationships will help to develop new beings in Christ, the supreme person who reveals God to man.

## PROJECTS FOR STUDY AND ACTION

1. Outline the steps in a process of group discussion. How may persons be helped at the various stages of the process? See pp. 68-84 in *Human Relations in Curriculum Change,* by K. D. Benne and Bozidar Muntyan.

2. Ask a group to plan the kind of worship experience that would help the following people gain some new insights into their relation to God. Role play the solutions.

*Case A: David Harum*

David Harum is a small businessman with a boy five years old. Suddenly the child dies. All during the child's lifetime the father had wanted to have him baptized, but the minister had failed to call on the father. When the child dies, David feels it is God's judgment upon him. He has a tremendous sense of guilt. He feels the church has let him down, that he has been rejected by the group. He says he will have nothing to do with the church. One day you meet him on the street. What would you say? What would you do? Why?

*Case B: Henry Irving*

Henry Irving is a gifted young educator who loves to champion causes. He has never faced the fact that his hidden motive in championing these causes is a feeling of hostility. It is one way in which he can express hostility before the whole group and still be in a position of leadership and accepted by the group.

One Sunday morning there is a sharp disagreement in the class discussion. The disagreement is dividing the class. How will you help redeem Henry in the midst of this disagreement? How do you handle this kind of conflict and direct it toward a redemptive end? Role play the solution.

### Case C: Mary Anderson

Mary Anderson grew up in a family of low income. All through her childhood her mother told her that she was an unwanted child. Very much rejected at home, she left home at the age of eighteen and married. Soon afterward she had a child.

Mary's husband comes and goes at will. The people in the community say he is not a very stable character. Mary is contemplating a divorce.

Mary tells a member of the group that she would like to come to one of the recreational events of the group.

How would you seek to relate yourself to Mary? If she came to the party, what would you do? What kind of recreation would you plan? Role play the solution.

3. Develop a worship experience that seeks to relate persons to God—to express the gratitude, find the guidance, or obtain the spiritual resources which they need.

## BIBLIOGRAPHY

1. Benne, K. D., and Muntyan, Bozidar. *Human Relations in Curriculum Change.* New York: Dryden Press, 1951. A collection of writings on the human relations factors in acquiring knowledge and learning values, skills, and relationships.
2. Brunner, Emil. *The Divine-Human Encounter.* Philadelphia: Westminster Press, 1943. A theological exposition of God's communication of His living word to man. Out of print.

3. Buber, Martin. *I and Thou.* New York: Chas. Scribner's Sons, 1937. A philosophical treatise on man's relation to man as a person, not a thing.
4. Cantor, Nathaniel. *The Teaching-Learning Process.* New York: Dryden Press, 1953. A description of the personal factors in learning in a reality-centered school.
5. "Christian Growth in Dynamic Groups," *International Journal of Religious Education,* XXXIII (May, 1957), 3-24. Penetrating insights by many authors on acceptance and rejection, participation, communication, and so on.
6. Foote, Nelson N., and Cottrell, Leonard S. *Identity and Interpersonal Competence.* Chicago: University of Chicago Press, 1955. A new study in family research based on competence in interpersonal relations.
7. Jenkins, D. H. "Planning Conditions for Personal Growth," *Adult Leadership,* II (February, 1954), 16-21. A good diagnostic check list for individual growth and insightful descriptions of the conditions in groups that aid personal growth.
8. Lewin, K., and Grabbe, P. "Problems of Re-Education," *Journal of Social Issues,* I (1945). Basic insights into ways persons change.
9. Lindgren, H. C. *The Art of Human Relations.* New York: Thomas Nelson & Sons, 1953. An analytic approach to communication and emotional maturity that affect interpersonal relations at work, in the family, and so on.
10. Marrow, A. J. *Living Without Hate.* New York: Harper & Bros., 1952. Contains "action research" by an industrial psychologist on ways of relieving tensions and minimizing hatred.
11. Maves, Paul. "Group Dynamics in the Class Room," *Religious Education,* XLVII (November-December, 1952), 381-86. An article describing basic principles and procedures in dynamic teaching.
12. Tillich, Paul. *The Courage to Be.* New Haven, Conn.: Yale University Press, 1952. Confronts our anxiety with the courage to stand alone and accept our dependence on God's creative power.

# CHAPTER VIII

# Commitment Is Decision with Depth

THE CLOSING SCENE OF THE PLAY "FAMILY PORTRAIT" IS PENE-trating. Mary and Joseph are trying to explain to Leban, a suitor of the younger sister of Jesus, what has happened to their son.

Joseph: And then he was always the guest of the local syna-gogue. He'd preach there on Sabbaths.

Leban: He was a rabbi?

Mary: Not a regular rabbi.

Simon: They called him that.

Mary: He wasn't interested in what people called him. That was one of the things he tried to teach his disciples. . . .

Leban: What did he teach?

Mary: Why—to—love your enemies—never to judge or con-demn anyone—to be *forgiving*. And to make life as easy as you could for other people. (*Pauses, groping for the most important things.*) To live for a purpose in which you believe and never let anyone keep you from your belief—not even your own family. You must be willing to die for it. And not to be afraid of people who—kill the body. Because, after that, there is nothing more they can do. (*A pause. . . .*) And to remember always that human life is beautiful—and noble—because it houses God. . . . I mean—when—when you degrade or dishonor human life—you degrade and dishonor God . . . (*Silence*) That was all he taught.

Leban: Has anyone ever tried it—to live the way he taught?

Mary: I don't think so.

Leban: Might be interesting to see what would happen if they did.[1]

It certainly might!

## Needed: Deeper Spiritual Perceptions

Such a quality of life requires a degree of commitment to Christ that cannot be attained in a twenty-minute interview, a thirty-minute study of a few Bible verses, or cursory discoursing about Christian concepts. Living by the Christian quality of life requires a depth of perception into the workings of the human spirit. It requires commitment-based decisions that involve this perception. It is not based upon our cultural concepts about Christ; it is based upon disciplined spiritual perceptions of faith, hope, and love. This marks the qualitative difference between learning about Christ and becoming an exponent of his way of life. This decision is made in the depths of a person's spirit.

Historically it is well to remember the Christian basis of commitment in religion. Commitment is not possible because Jesus taught some absolute ideals in the Sermon on the Mount and then left his disciples helpless to follow their impossible demands. Nor are Christians victims of some implacable web of fate which engulfed their cause when Jesus was crucified.

Jesus asserted, "I will not leave you comfortless." Then he gave them the gift of the Holy Spirit. This was not an emotional lift that would enable his followers to forget all their troubles. It was a continuing spiritual power that would reside in the lives of his people. Persons could discern it by

[1] By Lenore Coffee and William J. Cowen (Boston: Baker's Plays, 1940), pp. 126-128.

the fruits it produced in the lives of his followers. Paul described them: "love, joy, peace, patience, kindness, goodness, faithfulness, gentleness, self-control" (Gal. 5:22-25 R.S.V.). Persons whose lives were filled with these qualities were committed to the Christian way. The spirit which Christ gave to them was alive and working in them.

Psychologically it is well to remember that commitment is a necessary part of life. Much of the adjustment psychology of recent years obscured this fact. There was so much emphasis on adapting to one's environment that the deeper spiritual regions of man were obscured, his integrity threatened, and the possibilities of purposeful living obstructed by moral relativism.

## Commitment Is Central in Life

Yet commitment is central in the formation of personality. As Gardner Murphy points out:

Life depends, to a large degree, on relatively irreversible *commitments,* and each commitment constitutes a field. Many college men want at the same time to become doctors and to become lawyers. When a man decides at last what he is going to do, much of his personality is rapidly reworked. Old interests and attitudes drop out, and new ones are soon crystallized, and within a few years the regimentation of the professional attitude is practically absolute. Personality may be so deeply invaded by the outer situation that it can see no human problem from a non-professional point of view; we shudder at the very idea of an "unprofessional" outlook.

Field determination goes deep; and when once a commitment has been made, there is usually no possibility of going back to the unformed stage.[2]

[2] *Personality* (New York: Harper & Bros., 1947), pp. 888-89.

Perhaps our inability to distinguish between peripheral responses and real commitments has been due to our lack of understanding of the inner dynamics of the spirit of man. Kurt Lewin developed a concept of the "inner personal region" which gives a clue to the continuity and change that take place in our inner feelings, motives, and attitudes.

Dynamically the person appears as a "stratified" system which has a definite structure and in which one can distinguish central and peripheral regions. It has been shown that it is of great significance for problems of decision and intention, for questions of memory, of psychological satiation, of substitute satisfaction, and of emotion, whether the corresponding processes belong more to "peripheral" or to "central" regions.[3]

This inner personal region functions as a unity. New insights must be integrated into the whole field. Decisions with depth may cause the whole region to interact adaptively. Moreover, there is always tension between what is central and what is peripheral, and dynamic organization of these tensions brings the organism into an equilibrium. The directing of the central parts toward a goal may release tension or channel all one's energy in that direction.

"Man's dynamics, his creative vitality, is not undirected, chaotic, self-contained activity. It is directed, formed; it transcends itself toward meaningful contents," says Paul Tillich. "The dynamic character of being implies the tendency of everything to transcend itself and to create new forms."[4]

[3] *Principles of Topological Psychology* (New York: McGraw-Hill Book Co., 1936), p. 50.

[4] *Systematic Theology* (Chicago: University of Chicago Press, 1951), I, 180-81.

## Christian Commitment Defined

Commitment that is based upon the creative power of man's inner personal region rather than upon some peripheral response is not only more lasting; it is related to one's freedom and his power of becoming. This gives it a new dynamic character. Commitment is not simply conformity to some creedal formulation of the past. Christian commitment is linking the center of one's life, which guides the process of development, in a living, vital relationship to Christ and being guided by his spirit.

Decision and commitment are basic in the task of Christian education. Although the "inner personal region" is a field of forces in flux, there are definite configurations that represent a decision—a coming to fruition of a developmental process. It may represent an instant in time when one decides to live the Christian way. It may represent a revelation of thought when many ideas or insights break through one's consciousness in a meaningful way. It may represent a moment of awareness when a person comes to the realization that he is related to or has a common union with God. Persons have an integrity in their inner personal region. They are quite capable of making basic commitments about the life they will live.

## Groups Reinforce Decisions

The Christian group aids the person in making his basic decisions by opening a channel of energy and concern toward a new goal, about which the person has made a Christian value judgment. For the apostle Paul it involved saying, "This one thing I do." For us, this judgment is based upon a clear perception of the goal toward which we are striving. It involves insights into the next steps one wishes to take in moving toward this goal. It should be pointed out that this is a deeper response than a simple stimulus-response bond theory describes. With the group providing a climate that gives the individual a sense of stability, the intentional choice is not the product of frustration exercising itself in any kind of activity for release. The group not only has enabled the individual to clarify the goal toward which he seeks to strive; it is the base to which he returns to find spiritual renewal when his vocational efforts fail.

The religious significance of this development has been stated clearly by Fritz Künkel:

The power which moves us to love, to strive. . . . is the creative power of the ultimate end, the value ahead of us in the infinite future, drawing us like a magnet, training us, transforming us like a breeder who transforms flowers into more beautiful flowers. This power creates and forms for its inconceivable purposes, and, if we resist or try to escape, . . . we are corrected and, if necessary, remolded as the potter remolds his clay.

Such is the religious viewpoint which allows us for the first time in the history of science to work out a psychology applicable to individual life, and enables us at the same time to study and to influence the great collective powers of evolution and decay.[5]

The center of one's Christian faith is in the inner person. It is here that God the Creator is at work—in the soul of a man.

[5] *In Search of Maturity* (New York: Chas. Scribner's Sons, 1946), pp. 42-43.

## Groups Enhance Mental Health

In her study of groups Helen Jennings describes the fundamental differences between the "psychegroup" and the "sociogroup." The former is based upon congeniality of its members and exists to perform a function of clarification, security, and the enhancement of mental health of its members.

Psychegroups arise in all educational institutions and administrators of formal educational institutions, ignorant of their significance, usually tend either to ignore psychegroups among students, exhibit hostility toward them and attempt to destroy them, or to drive them "underground." As psychegroups are essential for mental health, all educational agencies have a responsibility for creating an atmosphere in which they can form and function freely, and for discouraging ways in which their creative energy can be integrated with the educational program.[6]

## Groups Implement Ethical Action

In contrast, the sociogroup seeks to get a job done. It defines goals and calls upon group members to make definite decisions and to take action.

In the experiments of Kurt Lewin in regard to leadership training, changing food habits, increasing work production, overcoming alcoholism, and eliminating race prejudice, he emphasized the fact that it is easier to change individuals within a group than it is to change them separately. As long as the values of the group remain unchanged, the individual will resist any attempt to deviate from the group standard. If through the process of group thinking and group decision

[6] *Adult Education,* October, 1947, pp. 178-79.

the standard of values for the whole group may be altered, the resistance of the individuals to any kind of change will be lessened considerably.

In the growth and development of adult groups within the Christian church, the leaders must determine the nature of their groups. In my opinion a fellowship of Christians can perform both functions. There are times and occasions when the group needs to be carrying out the functions of a psychegroup. This is a redemptive function. There are times when it would be a sociogroup, seeking to discover the ethical goals of Christianity, making group decisions, and taking group action that would bring about conditions in human relations wherein the kingdom of God may come among men.

There was a very close interrelation between these two functions in the strategy of Jesus. Before encouraging persons to participate in the temple worship, he instructed them to visit their neighbors and to establish just relationships with them. Then they could participate in the temple worship.

A part of the devitalizing process that goes on in any group is reached when its activities become routine. Week in and week out, it is the same thing. Persons know what will take place before they go to the meeting. In a dynamic group both the redemption of individuals and group decision that leads to ethical action will be carried out as a result of the therapeutic and the thought process that goes on within the fellowship of the group.

When a group begins to "center down" on a goal that it thinks is worth moving toward, the members share their convictions. They begin to get down to the inner core of their own beings. Beliefs count now, beliefs on which they are willing to stake their lives or their futures. If their insights cannot stand this test, if they do not inhere with a person's own integrity, they should reject the ideas.

## The Commitment Process

This centering down process involves the person in the depths of his soul. Here commitment takes place. People speak only out of their innermost convictions.

At this point it is necessary for other members of the group to discipline themselves so that they may participate with wisdom and understanding. They need to listen to each other with patience and insight. Some persons may be exploring new possibilities. Vehemence of utterance may reveal the conflict within a soul. They need others who will listen until they clarify their new insights. The use of hatred or fear to enforce commitment can scar and distort the inner personal region. Immediately they can begin to relay peripheral responses. They may yield to group pressure but yielding temporarily is not commitment. It can even be a form of escape. Commitment is a free, voluntary action in which a person takes responsibility for redirecting his own life toward the Christ-centered goal that has been revealed to him.

When a person is in the process of making a commitment to Christ and the Christian way of life, the members of the group need to communicate their own personal faith. They speak after they have given the Holy Spirit a chance in their own souls. Rather than make the decision for the other person, they seek to set up the conditions wherein he can make his own decision. Alternatives must be clarified, implications discerned. Experiences must be shared and biblical truths made relevant. Pertinent facts and knowledge must be shared so that the person may use them to make a decision. When this is done with skill, the person feels a new release of spiritual power. When it is done without threatening his soul, he acquires new spiritual health. He is whole again. He becomes a channel through which the love of God operates in the world. He is a new center of dynamic spiritual power, out from which a Christian influence may be transmitted.

## PROJECTS FOR STUDY AND ACTION

1. Choose any biblical material you desire. Work out a teaching plan for a lesson. The purpose of this lesson is to get persons to commit their lives to Christ.

2. List and demonstrate a procedure that makes it impossible for commitment to take place.

3. Give a demonstration of "peripheral response" and "depth response" to the same question.

4. How would you proceed in leading a discussion so that persons may be guided by the Holy Spirit? How would you keep the group under control all the time?

5. Write out a statement contrasting a "psychegroup" with a "sociogroup."

6. Demonstrate with the assistance of two classmates one procedure in helping a group clarify its goals.

7. Demonstrate one procedure in helping a group make a decision.

8. Demonstrate the way you would assist a person in making a commitment to Christ without the use of hatred or fear.

# BIBLIOGRAPHY

1. Boisen, Anton T. *The Exploration of the Inner World.* New York: Willett, Clark & Co., 1937. A pioneer treatment of depth psychology.
2. Casteel, John. *Spiritual Renewal Through Personal Groups.* New York: Association Press, 1957. A fascinating description of the power of small groups to renew the life of men and women today.
3. Howe, R. L. "The Theological Aspects of Commitment," *Religious Education,* LI (July-August, 1956), 290-97. An article discussing our relationship of trust in God.
4. James, William. *The Varieties of Religious Experience.* New York: Modern Library. The classic description of the varieties of manifestations of religious experiences in our time.
5. Lewin, Kurt. "Forces Behind Food Habits and Methods of Change." *Bulletin of the National Research Council,* 1943, pp. 35-65. A documented study of factors prevailing in changing attitudes and food habits during wartime.
6. Lewin, Kurt. "Group Decision and Social Change," *Readings in Social Psychology,* ed. Newcomb, T. M., and Hartley, E. L. New York: Henry Holt & Co., 1947. A description of the process of group decision as a force for social change.
7. Outler, A. C. *Psychotherapy and the Christian Message.* New York: Harper & Bros., 1954. Explores the relationship of Christian thought to the findings of psychotherapy.
8. Roberts, David E. *Psychotherapy and a Christian View of Man.* New York: Chas. Scribner's Sons, 1951. A correlating of the psychotherapeutic and the Christian view of man.
9. Wise, Carroll A. *Psychiatry and the Bible.* New York: Harper & Bros., 1956. An interpretation of the problems of mental health through analysis of persons in the Bible.
10. Zeigler, J. H. "Psychological Aspects of Commitment," *Religious Education,* LI (July-August, 1956), 298-307. Discusses commitment from the point of view of dynamic field theory psychology.

# CHAPTER IX

# Leadership and Membership in Adult Groups

HARRY OVERSTREET TELLS A FASCINATING STORY ABOUT GOING to speak at a college commencement. On the subway he sat down beside an Italian family that was all dressed up for a special occasion. He noticed that their excitement increased as they rode along, so he asked, "What's the trouble?"

"My son graduates from college today," the father replied, "and we are not sure of the way to get there."

Overstreet told them that he was going to the same place and would take them to the college. When he arrived at the auditorium, he directed them to good seats where they could witness the proceedings. Then he slipped backstage.

After the exercises Overstreet returned to his new friends. Joy and elation reigned supreme among the members of the family who had sacrificed to put the eldest son through college. Other relatives had joined the celebration. When the proud father saw Overstreet, he beckoned to the eminent educator and said, "Come meet my friend." Expecting some comment on his address, Overstreet was surprised when the overjoyed father introduced him to the friends with these words, "I want you to meet my friend. He is the man who showed us the way."

## Leadership Described

Perhaps this is the highest compliment that can be paid to a leader. He is a person who has been over the path of knowledge until he has mastered the way. He is thoroughly familiar with the ways adults learn. He can guide persons in their search for truth. He is sensitive to the needs of persons and responds to them at their own level of development. He has a way of stimulating interaction between persons so that they may help one another. He knows how to communicate his feeling of confidence, mutual trust, and the desire to discover new knowledge. Thus, a leader of adult groups in the church not only has a mastery of biblical knowledge; he can relate that knowledge to their needs. He not only has a mastery of theological beliefs; he can prompt a response of mutual trust and faith. He not only has a close personal relationship with Christ which surpasses the facts he relates about Christ; he can lead others into a personal experience of this relation to Christ and show them the way to more abundant Christian living.

## Goals of Leadership

In times past, leaders of adults in the church conceived of their task as making up for deficiencies in religious knowledge. If laymen were lacking in biblical information, leaders of adult classes conceived their purpose to be imparting biblical history and fact. Naturally the leader would have his anxiety heightened when persons in the class asked him questions to which he did not know the answers. This possibility would tend to cause the leader to restrict his way of working with a group. Changes in ways of operating would seem to threaten him because persons might ask embarrassing questions. He conceived his leadership to be based upon the fact that it was his task to impart information which members of the class did not know.

The leader in an adult class in the church was not alone in this notion. Educators in the field of secular adult education built their approach upon the notion that they were to help persons make up for something they had missed along the way. For example, much adult education was for persons who were illiterate so that they could learn to read and write. A great deal of adult education was conducted in the cities for immigrants so that they might become citizens of their newly chosen country.

Today, however, a demand for more and more learning shows clearly that millions of adults who have had at least a high school education want to learn more. They are not simply making up for deficiencies. They want to participate in a full, rich, and abundant life through the joy of study. This demand calls for rethinking some of the primary aims of leadership in secular education and in the church school.

## A Means to the Abundant Life

Christian adult education can now become the means to the full, wholesome, moral, and spiritual development that leads to the abundant life for millions of Americans who are forever learning. The rise of lay leadership in the churches during the past few years has hastened the day when they can share the rich storehouse of their own experiences.

These persons need to plan so that they learn much more from one another. Leaders need to plan, with spirit-led imaginations, a great variety of new programs that will meet the emerging demands of adults. These laymen are capable of initiating new approaches to these educational needs that will surpass any attempts that have been made in the past. Rather than feel that his leadership is threatened, the new leader needs to develop the attitude that he is a fellow learner among equals and to proceed in such a way as to enable each person to contribute on the basis of his experience, knowledge, insight, and understanding.

Leadership is a process of mutual stimulation and interaction between maturing adults which enhances the action toward their chosen goals. In a Christian group leaders will assist by helping the group define the problems or the areas of concern which they desire to explore. They will assist them in clarifying the goals they seek. They will bring information, share experiences, conduct research, make reports so that the group will have adequate information with which to work. They will seek to summarize, make decisions, plan programs of ethical action in keeping with the Christian insights and understandings that they have learned. They will seek to carry out the redemptive function within the group that enables persons to become related to God, to Christ, and to their fellow men in a wholesome, life-sustaining way. As members of the group learn how to perform these tasks, the leadership in the group may move from one person to many persons who, on the basis of their insights, make a responsible contribution that is needed in the situation in which they are involved.

## Members' Obligations

As members of adult groups in the churches become more aware of their leadership obligations, they will need to become more sensitive to and skillful in the distinctive functions of group leadership. As they assume responsibility for their own growth and development, they will not look to the leader to start every discussion. They will choose their own curriculum; they will participate in formulating the aims of the group; they will begin to discuss by asking questions and addressing their statements to one another, rather than to the leader each time as if asking for permission to speak. Nor will they depend upon the leader as an oracle who is final arbiter in all disputes. They will seek to create a climate of freedom in which persons can explore the real issues that plague their minds. They believe and accept the doubter, love and trust the persons who ask embarrassing questions, and they will seek to work with the problem persons in constructive ways. They will be free enough to say, "I believe; help thou mine unbelief." They will not feel that they are under the threat of "Believe it this way or be damned." They will not force persons to check all their doubts outside the classroom so that when they come in they must conform to whatever the strongest person has to say. That kind of group idolatry will meet with the same fate as Aaron's calf in a mature group where persons are free and responsible.

In a Christian group in which members have had a part in determining their own group goal they will feel the need for participation. As they grow in maturity as members of the group, they will bring information, share experiences, make reports on research. They will not depend upon one of the "bright boys" to bring in all this data. They will seek to assist one another by listening, by asking questions that clarify the thoughts of the others, and by adding information that makes these ideas more meaningful and practical.

Through this educational process the member of the group continuously identifies the goals of the gospel with the goals of his life and seeks to make those changes in his life so that he may measure up to the goals of the gospel more closely.

## Right Relationships a Primary Function

Throughout this development members of the group need to become much more aware of their relationship to others as persons. Group-centered leadership is primarily a matter of interpersonal relationships. As individuals master these face-to-face relationships, they learn how to relate themselves to God and to their fellow men. In this way they are fulfilling the injunction of Jesus to "love the Lord thy God with all thy heart, mind, soul, and strength, and thy neighbor as thyself."

Jesus had a remarkable capacity for restoring persons to this kind of right relationship to God and to their fellow men. The Samaritan woman had built up barriers of distrust for other persons; Jesus restored her to her right relationship with God in one of the most insightful passages in the New Testament on the ways in which we worship God as spirit, and then he set her about the task of restoring a right relationship with her fellow men. The Gerasene demoniac suffered a split personality under the duress of the times in which he lived; Jesus restored him to a new wholeness of spirit and a new relationship to the men in the town who had cast him out. Zacchaeus felt his inferiority deeply; he exploited his countrymen to compensate for it. Jesus established a redemptive relationship with him, enabling him to live with his fellow men in a reconciled and helpful way. If members are going to assume new responsibilities for the full and abundant life, they must relate themselves to Christ in a believing and life-sustaining way. Nurturing this vital relationship is the primary function of the Christian community.

As adults experience this kind of dynamic Christian learning more and more, changes will take place in their lives. They will not be learning the Bible simply as words; it will become the living word which will live within them, guiding and motivating their thoughts and their actions toward other people. They will seek to communicate to others the way of life which they experience and understand. Thus the Christian group will become a redemptive fellowship in which persons who are related to God, to Christ, and to their fellow men in a wholesome way will find their true worth as spiritual beings who are God-inspired and spirit-led. These changes will come about through self-discipline based upon spiritual insights.

## Change Through Self-Discipline

If we are to move toward a more dynamic concept of Christian adult education, leaders and members of adult groups will need to change voluntarily under their own self-discipline. These changes will be a very gradual process based upon the learning of many new insights and skills. They will come about as persons understand what they are doing, try new procedures, and see that the results are an improvement over the old ways of doing things. After new insights and skills are tested, they must be related to the previous experience of the person in such a way as to make that previous experience more meaningful and worthwhile. Gradually, through self-discipline, we can begin to control our attitudes toward others. We can control those strong desires toward selfishness that give us a false sense of security, those prejudices that give us a false sense of superiority, and those hatreds that give us a false sense of power. In these relationships, we seek to follow the spirit of Christ. Here is the key to the inner disciplines for leaders and members of adult groups in the church.

This kind of inner discipline is related to the process of becoming mature Christians. It is a vital and intentional process whereby persons are guided by the spirit of Christ. It is the process by which men and women who are related to God seek to discover the meaning of Christ for their personal lives, accept his love, power, and truth, and seek to establish a continuing and living relationship with him.

This does not mean learning to live a relaxed and complacent life. It means living under tension as we realize how far we fall short of the expectations of Christ every day. It does not mean simply living by the release of something in man's chaotic subconsciousness, *à la* Freud. It means living under the guidance of the spirit of Christ and changing on the basis of new insights which his spirit reveals to us.

## Toward Mature Participation

Carroll A. Wise of Garrett Biblical Institute has explained this concept of mature Christian living in a pungent and clarifying way.

It involves a living relationship with other persons and with God in Christ through which we find strength to face and accept painful reality and to respond in love and trust. This requires giving up our childish insistence that life be "happy"; giving up any desire to suffer for the sake of suffering and getting sympathy; being willing to face and resolve those painful elements in our experience which can be resolved; and learning to live constructively with those elements which cannot be resolved. Insofar as the church helps us to do this, it is contributing to the maturing and fulfillment of our personalities, and helping us attain genuine wholeness.[1]

In the process of becoming Christian we are being Christian.

Basically the Christian life is a life of faith. Although this faith has rational content, it is not fully guided by rational evidence. It transcends rational thought. The man of faith uses symbols to express truths that are infinite in scope, duration, and meaning. They transcend sense data, the logic of the customary, and the norms set by mathematical *quanta*. They are known through insight and intuition. The life of faith involves both *risk* (Abraham went forth, not knowing where) and *doubt* ("I believe; help thou mine unbelief"), for it is a life of ultimate concern about our relationship to God.

## Summary

Mature leaders and members of adult groups in the church will:

1. create a climate of Christian fellowship in their group
2. listen with understanding to the contributions of others
3. assist the group in clarifying alternatives, making decisions, proposing plans
4. delegate authority to others and trust in their creative ability to get things done
5. be aware of personal needs of others and seek to respond in a Christian way

[1] *Psychiatry and the Bible* (New York: Harper & Bros., 1956), p. 135.

6. keep growing as they gain insights, test experiences, use their best spiritual and ethical judgments, and change as they work out a better way of living together.

## PROJECTS FOR STUDY AND ACTION

1. Role play three different types of leaders of a group.
2. Role play different ways members participate in a productive group.
3. What is group leadership? (See *Adult Leadership*, June, 1952, pp. 13-20, and *Group Leadership and Democratic Action*, F. S. Haiman.)
4. Ask members of the group to practice some group disciplines. Instead of arguing with a person who is confused, practice saying the words that will give him reassurance.
5. Interview a group leader concerning the way he views himself. (Circle appraisal.)

| | |
|---|---|
| a) listens with understanding | 5 4 3 2 1 |
| b) supports members | 5 4 3 2 1 |
| c) delegates authority | 5 4 3 2 1 |
| d) capacity to change and grow | 5 4 3 2 1 |
| e) brings out the best in others | 5 4 3 2 1 |

Later interview five members of the group concerning the way they regard him. Compare the two reports.

### BIBLIOGRAPHY

1. Cartwright, Dorwin, and Zander, Alvin. *Group Dynamics*. Evanston, Ill.: Row, Peterson & Co., 1953. Advanced reading. A collection of the basic findings of research in group dynamics. For leaders who have a background of understanding.
2. Frank, Lawrence K. *How to Be a Modern Leader*. New York:

Association Press, 1954. Delineates the special functions of a leader as a member of the group.

3. *Groups, Leadership and Men.* Ed. Harold Guetzkow. New Brunswick, N. J.: Rutgers University Press, 1951. Pp. 119-58 especially on leadership.

4. Gordon, Thomas. *Group-Centered Leadership.* Boston: Houghton Mifflin Co., 1955. A discussion of group-centered leadership and an analysis of the workshop way of developing it.

5. Lippitt, Ronald, and Zander, Alvin. "Sharing the Leadership Load," *Adult Leadership,* I (June, 1952), 13-20. An article analyzing the functions of leadership in a group.

6. Strauss, Bert and Frances. *New Ways to Better Meetings.* New York: Viking Press, 1951. A popular treatment of new procedures in working with groups. See ch. XV, "Stimulating Change."

7. *Training Group Leaders* (pamphlet). Chicago: Adult Education Association of U.S.A., 1955. A series of articles describing the functions of leadership, the role of the trainer, the training process, and measuring leadership performance.

8. "Training in Member Roles," *Adult Leadership,* I (January, 1953), 17-23. A popular and graphic description of ways to train members to participate in a group. Easy to read.

9. Wittenberg, Rudolph M. *The Art of Group Discipline.* New York: Association Press, 1951. A practical volume which discusses the ways groups can work out their own problems in self-discipline.

# CHAPTER X

# Maturing as Christians

CERTAINLY ONE OF THE PURPOSES OF CHRISTIAN ADULT
education is to help persons attain maturity in the Christian
way of living. They need to make moral choices in the light
of the basic Christian norms and motives. They need to bring
the redemptive resources of our religion to bear upon life's
interpersonal and intergroup relationships.

*Becoming Mature Christians*

This kind of maturity is facilitated when adults face the
developmental tasks of life with a Christian spirit. Failing to
meet the moral and social demands placed upon them because of their age, sex, occupation, family roles, community
needs, and organizational memberships, they become cases
of arrested development. Only as they become capable of
making Christian choices daily and apply the redemptive
spirit in life's relationship, can they grow into the fullness of
the maturity of Christ.

*Love as Norm and Motive*

It is readily accepted among Christians that God expects
us to live a life that is guided by love. "Thou shalt love the
Lord thy God with all thy heart, mind, soul, and strength,
and thy neighbor as thyself," said Jesus, as he quoted the
Hebrew Shema. They are all given talents, capacities, and

potentialities. With these powers that can be developed, they can respond to the love of God in difficult and complex situations.

Fortunately or unfortunately, the church attracts persons who are having a hard time trying to mature on the basis of this principle. Some of them have such a possessive love that they would smother every effort of children to learn the Christian way of life for themselves. They want to do it for them. They tell them what to think and when to think it until all the creative lure of adventure and discovery is stifled in them. Others come to the church to isolate themselves from society. Here they know they will be received and accepted. Usually they try to use the church as a sounding board for their ethical superiority over the pagans on the outside. Both of these types of persons want to remain just as they are, yet both must change if they are going to grow toward the maturity that we find in Christ.

Adults need the help and guidance of the church in facing the major changes in life. Sometimes they pass through periods of tremendous inner conflict as they seek to work out their ways of life in the face of new possible roles. Just what is the place of a woman in our society? Should this question be decided by economic standards predominantly? Should she be a career woman, or a housewife, or both? How much responsibility should she take in society? In the church? How much should she stay at home? Is the husband's role merely that of breadwinner and the wife's that of caring for the children? Does the husband have some responsibility for the children and does the wife's "good housekeeping" extend to the community too? No easy answer to these questions can be formulated.

The family is changing. It is no longer an authoritarian society where father is the "autocrat of the breakfast table," nor
is it a closely knit economic society where people are held
together for survival because here is where they grow the
wool that is made into clothes and grow the food that keeps
body and soul together. The family is shifting to a more
spiritual basis for its cohesiveness. Here is where persons
learn to grow in love and affection toward one another. This
task is now primary.

And where can adults get help in learning how to become
more mature in their love for each other and their children?
If any agency in society can help them, it should be the
church. It should know more about the love of God than any
other agency on earth. It should be able to guide persons in
finding mature ways of being channels for the love of God
in their human relationships. Potentially, the church has
what they need.

This kind of guidance comes to a person as he learns how
to change through self-control and to master life's relationships. This is precisely the spot where we need to take a new
look at the adult education program of the church.

One day in a pastors' meeting a minister spoke out, saying,
"I get my young adults into the work of the church as quickly
as possible. That's my program of adult education." He meant
that they would learn the work of the church best by doing it.

Of course he was right as far as he went, but the work of
the church is more than budgets and financial campaigns,
more than worship services and getting new members, more
than service projects and missions. The church's work is
*redemptive*. It is possible for a person to champion a cause of
the church, to ride herd on the whole congregation, to exceed

the quotas required, and still not communicate the love of God toward people in the process.

Christ had compassion on people. That is why he helped them. Our service in the church must be the means of communicating our compassion for others. This requires learning the "language of relationships"—treating people as persons, not manipulating them as things. Else, what does it profit if we raise every budget and lose the redemptive spirit?

Every experience in adult groups is a learning opportunity, a chance to become a more mature Christian. We need to plan with other persons so that they may have this opportunity.

## Negotiating Developmental Tasks

Listening is not enough; people change through participation. As they learn to negotiate their developmental tasks in a spirit of Christian love, they become wholesome and mature. As they fail or are rejected, they submerge these hurts into lower levels of consciousness. These emotionalized factors then become hidden motives that determine the way they react toward life. Recognition of these developmental factors in adulthood will go a long way toward putting adult education in the church on a more sound basis.

## Tasks of Young Adulthood

Young adulthood is a time of new beginnings. It is a time when a person leaves his family and his home and starts out into adult life on his own. Here he must learn how to get along with his employer and with the other employees. This work group will have a tremendous influence upon his moral standards and his spiritual hopes. It may set the attitudes in terms of which he makes many of his life's choices.

Young adulthood is the time when persons get married and begin to set up homes of their own. According to the many choices they make, this relationship will either be a continuous source of happiness and spiritual power or will be a rocky road to ruin. In young adulthood the first children are born and parents must learn the art and responsibilities of child care, nurture, and development. It is here that they must learn to make a reasonable and Christian accommodation to the limitations of the infant as the child develops in the family. This is a difficult and self-discipling task. It will affect the whole process of setting the children free. It will affect the way the children meet crises in their own lives.

As young adults vote, as they pay taxes, as their children associate with other children, as they assume responsibilities in the community, they enter into new relationships with the social, political, and economic institutions in community life. Here larger social and ethical implications begin to emerge. They begin to think about extending a Christian influence into their relationships in groups of people and institutions in society. The psychologist E. H. Erikson points out that here young adults may decide whether they will be outgoing or whether they will withdraw and be isolationist in their attitudes toward life. Quite frequently the patterns for the rest of their lives are set during young adulthood.

It is interesting to note that in tests of their scales of values young adults put security—economic security—at the top of the list of values for which they will strive in life. In contrast, the older adults place love, affection, and friends at the top of their list as those values to be most desired and sought after in life. Perhaps it takes a great deal of living to discern these values and to appraise rightly their real merit.

## Duties of the Middle-aged

Middle age is the period of heaviest responsibility. Here is carried the economic load. The children make great economic demands upon their parents. It is estimated that it takes nearly fourteen thousand dollars per child to get them through high school these days. The middle-aged person is buying his home, buying large chunks of life insurance, and trying to acquire enough money to get his child or children through college. Perhaps the care of elderly parents presses in upon him also, and he must carry this heavier burden for a while.

In middle life we face life's dead ends. We begin to see that we have our limitations. The person who thought he would be bank president now comes to realize that he will never be more than a bank teller. His income begins to level off and he cannot look forward to greater increases. Women discover that they are never going to have children and that they must make a reasonable and Christian adjustment to this situation.

During these years, adults face the fact of bereavement in a very personal way. It is at this time that they usually lose their parents, and the questions of life and death take on much more serious meaning than they have before. Perhaps this prompts them to probe more deeply, to discover for themselves a philosophy of life that will give meaning and value to their own existence. They face this primary existential question, "What shall I do to make life more fruitful?" It is during these years that a person comes to his full maturity, to the full development of his powers in terms of both knowledge and experience. From now on he will be going downhill. He must find a sense of fulfillment for his life.

The young adult can get by with enthusiasm and hope. The middle-aged adult must discern that life has meaning and purpose. This is especially true when the last child leaves home. After years of struggle and sacrifice that have been completely absorbing for the mother, and emotionally, as well as financially, involving for the father, a feeling of loneliness and emptiness can come over their lives as the last child leaves. With time on their hands the question keeps coming to mind, "Was it worth it?" The way they answer that question will determine the way they act from now on. It causes some persons to go on a spree. It causes others to live as nomads, seeking to escape from the rest of life.

It is here and now that these persons need the help of the church as they have never needed it before. If life is to take on new meaning, they must rediscover its spiritual meanings and purposes. The adult educational groups of the church can help if their leaders discern the developmental tasks of these persons. If we obscure these tasks, if we proceed as if the Bible is unrelated to them, these persons will become arrested in their development. As a result, the church may have on its hands persons who declare that the love of God is a completely otherworldly thing with no relevance for their lives here and now. Or these persons can become channels through which God can work to serve in the community. With their new leisure they can help in hospitals, work with children and youth, and bring the wisdom of their mature years to bear upon the many ministries of the church.

*Old Age: Fulfillment or Regret?*

During older adulthood, life closes in on the person. He may come to this realization suddenly, in a crisis, when he is forced to retire at a certain age. He feels healthy, he feels capable, but the time has come when his fruitful days of working are at an end. One morning he finds a pink slip on his desk and goes to the office window to get his retirement check and to work out his arrangements with the Social Security office. The older adult, from this point on, finds that his economic opportunities are limited greatly.

Life closes in when a husband dies and the woman, who usually lives about six or seven years longer than the man, finds that she no longer has a mate by her side; her lifelong companion has slipped away. Loneliness is a very difficult problem. It takes all of one's faith to overcome it. It does queer things to people. It is hard to cope with. It makes one feel that life is really closing in on a person.

In old age persons must learn how to simplify life. They can no longer keep up the many recreational activities which formerly enticed them. They can no longer keep up the many social contacts which they have had; yet they have time, lots of time, on their hands. It seems wonderful at first but after a while it becomes a drudgery, and life is a bore.

During these later years some organ of the body may fail and persons must learn how to live with only part of a body or with an organ that is only partially functioning. This is a source of despair and disillusionment to many older persons.

Older adults want to be loved and they want to be useful, but life seems to have closed in on them and they lose out in both of these areas unless they have built adequate inner resources to meet this developmental task of old age.

In Protestant Christian education we believe that all members of the adult group are a part of the priesthood of believers. They can minister to the needs of one another. As a person faces one of these developmental tasks, he may seek the guidance of another who is a little more mature. One who has passed through this same kind of experience can show how the Christian gospel is relevant to the tasks of the mature years. He can explain how he made his choice or how his experience was reinforced by a resolve of the will to live by a moral standard which the church has taught. In this way the church helps older adults seek to attain the fullness of the maturity of Christ. The degree to which it succeeds will determine whether old age is a time of fulfillment or of regret.

*Summary: "The Measure of the Stature of . . . Christ"*

If adults are going to mature as Christians, we need to make a dynamic approach to the tasks of adult education in the churches.

1. We must seek to make the adult groups a fellowship of love and understanding. Persons cannot learn the Christian way of life in an environment where the opposite prevails.

2. We need to understand the roles that are necessary for a group to function well and encourage our members to participate. Persons change when they are accepted in a group and when they can participate in it.

3. The more mature members of the group need to learn new disciplines:

    *a*) Accepting others who disagree with their ideas

*b*) Listening to the other person until they understand the condition of his soul

*c*) Changing under their own self-discipline

4. We need to realize that religious learning involves more than the mastery of biblical and theological ideas. It involves relationships. We seek to relate persons to God through Christ who became a person and lived among us. We have a living relationship with his spirit to guide us in managing life's relationships.

5. We need to rely on the guidance of the Holy Spirit. We bring the problems and baffling circumstances of life into the classroom, seek the guidance of others, pray together, clarify issues and choices, and receive the further insight that comes through God's revealing power. We have a living faith.

6. John Wesley once said, "Let us unite the two so long divided: knowledge and vital piety." In this spirit we continue to use the intelligence of the best-informed minds, ideas conveyed through the printed page, audio-visual resources that bring vivid images of people from many lands, field trips, interviews, and service projects, so that persons may have a steady stream of information upon which to base their reflections and choices.

7. Adult groups need to become little laboratories in which we test the power to create "the good" and to redeem the lives of persons. Here is where the unloved, the egoist, the hate-filled person has a chance to come under the influence of the Christian spirit and to feel the urge to become whole again.

Although we fail many times, these things we must do,

until we all attain to the unity of the faith and of the knowledge of the Son of God, to mature manhood, to the measure of the stature of the fullness of Christ; so that we may no longer be children, tossed to and fro and carried about by every wind of doctrine, by the cunning of men, by their craftiness in deceitful wiles. Rather, speaking the truth in love, we are to grow up in every way into him who is the head, into Christ, from whom the whole body, joined and knit together by every joint with which it is supplied when each part is working properly, makes bodily growth and upbuilds itself in love. (Eph. 4:13-16. R.S.V.)

## PROJECTS FOR STUDY AND ACTION

1. What is your understanding of the way maturity takes place in adult life? See *Personality*, by Gardner Murphy, pp. 619-62, and *Religious Education*, XLVI (September-October, 1951), 271-92.

2. What is your understanding of the term "developmental tasks"? See pp. 126 and 129. See also *Human Development and Education*, by R. J. Havighurst.

3. Chart the "developmental tasks" of young adults, middle-aged adults, and older adults.

4. Trace one set of tasks through the adult years, showing the distinctive tasks at each stage of development.

5. Analyze the study and activities of an adult group. How have they helped the members face or solve their own "developmental tasks"?

6. Cite any examples of ways adults have faced these tasks and worked them out satisfactorily through the help of members in an adult group.

7. As a result of this study, what changes would you institute in the groups in which you serve and share?

# BIBLIOGRAPHY

1. Allport, G. W. *Personality: A Psychological Interpretation.* New York: Henry Holt and Co., 1937. A basic psychological study of personality.

2. Baruch, Dorothy. *New Ways in Discipline.* New York: McGraw-Hill Book Co., 1949. An excellent treatment of the theory that self-discipline is the best discipline.

3. Dunbar, Flanders. *Mind and Body.* New York: Random House, 1947. A study of psychosomatic relationships in the human organism.

4. Havighurst, R. J. *Human Development and Education.* New York: Longmans, Green & Co., 1953. A fundamental analysis of the developmental tasks of childhood, adolescence, and adulthood.

5. Hiltner, Seward. *Self-Understanding.* New York: Charles Scribner's Sons, 1951. For purposes of self-analysis. Good biblical illustrations.

6. Jung, C. G. *Modern Man in Search of a Soul.* New York: Harcourt, Brace & Co., 1955. A study of analytical psychology: dream analysis, the unconscious, and the relation of psychology to religion.

7. Künkel, Fritz. *In Search of Maturity.* New York: Charles Scribner's Sons, 1943. The relation of depth psychology to self-education is discussed from a religious perspective.

8. Lawton, George. *Aging Successfully.* New York: Columbia University Press, 1946. A standard treatment of the problems and the process of aging.

9. Maynard, D. M. *Your Home Can Be Christian.* Nashville: Abingdon Press, 1952. The problems of family life examined from a Christian point of view.

10. Maves, Paul B. *The Best Is Yet to Be.* Philadelphia: Westminster Press, 1951. An excellent discussion of the problems of older adulthood. Devotionally written.

11. Murphy, Gardner. *Personality.* New York: Harper & Bros., 1947. The most comprehensive treatment of personality in our time. A biosocial approach.

12. Overstreet, H. A. *The Mind Alive.* New York: W. W. Norton & Co., 1954. Handling our emotions in times of duress and crisis is discussed with insight and wisdom.

13. "Research Findings on Human Development," *Religious Education,* XLVI (September-October, 1951), 271-92. A short review of

some of the most significant findings in the current studies of human development.

14. Rogers, C. R. *Counseling and Psychotherapy*. Boston: Houghton Mifflin Co., 1942. A description of the nondirective approach in counseling.

15. Sherrill, L. J. *The Gift of Power*. New York: Macmillan Co., 1955. An insightful discussion of the place of the Holy Spirit in Christian education.

16. Sherif, M., and Cantril, H. *Psychology of Ego-Involvements*. New York: John Wiley & Sons, 1947. A basic study of the new approach to ego involvement in human motivation.

# *Index*

Holy Spirit
  and the church, 80
  gift of, 92, 105
  promptings of, 80
*Human Development and Education,* 136
*Human Relations,* 33
*Human Relations and Curriculum Change,* 101
*Human Use of Human Beings, The,* 22-23

*I and Thou,* 26, 93
*In Search of Maturity,* 109
Incarnation
  as God in communication, 80
  meaning of, 80, 92
"Inner personal region," 107
Interaction, 35, 38
International Lesson Series, 84
Irrelevancy, as barrier to communication, 80-81

Jacob and Esau, 67
Jennings, Helen, 110
Jesus Christ
  and the disciples, 30
  and the Gerasene demoniac, 97-98, 120
  and the Great Commandment, 120
  his reconciling relationship to man, 98-99
  incarnation as communication, 80
  Lord's Prayer, the, 86
  meaning of suffering of, 85-86
  "measure of stature of," 134-36
  parables of, 66, 82
  redemptive function of, 83, 120-21
  resurrection of, 85

Jesus Christ—*cont'd*
  and the Samaritan woman, 120
  and Zacchaeus, 98, 120
Jones, E. Stanley, 87
Joseph and brothers, 50

Kagawa, Toyohiko, 87
Künkel, Fritz, 109

Lashley, K. S., 25
Leadership
  of adults, 123
  in autocratic atmosphere, 33-34
  description of, 116
  goals of, 116-17
  with group as center, 120-21
  laymen in, 117-18
  as process, 117-18
Learning
  as change through self-discipline, 75-76, 91, 121
  of the Christian way of life, 14, 25, 91
  conditioned reflex theory of, 22-23
  definition of, 91
  dynamic approach to, 24-28
  foundation for, 92
  insight in, 26-27
  for lifetime, 12, 126-34
  motivation for, 46
  as personal encounter, 25, 93-99
Lecture process, 66
Leisure, as way to abundant life, 13
Lewin, Kurt
  on group climate, 33
  on "inner personal region," 107
  on "peripheral and central regions" concept, 107

141